COLLECTING VICTORIAN PORCELAIN

Collecting
Victorian Porcelain

ERNEST REYNOLDS

FREDERICK A. PRAEGER, *Publishers*

New York · Washington

BOOKS THAT MATTER

Published in the United States of America in 1968
by Frederick A. Praeger, Inc., Publishers
111 Fourth Avenue, New York, N.Y. 10003

© 1966 in London, England, by Ernest Reynolds

Library of Congress Catalog Card Number: 68–16721

Printed in Great Britain

ACKNOWLEDGEMENTS

I wish to thank all those who have generously helped me in the preparation of this book, especially in connection with the illustrations.

I am particularly grateful to Mr J. E. Hartill, the Managing Director of Mintons, for permission to reproduce some of the splendid specimens of Victorian porcelain in the Minton Works Museum, and also for his very great kindness in making my visit to Stoke-on-Trent so enjoyable. I am also much indebted to Mr H. Holdway and Messrs Copeland for their most valuable help in allowing pictures of their fine historical collection to appear in this book, and to Mr A. R. Mountford, Curator of the Hanley Museum and Art Gallery, for similar permission.

Mr Cyril Shingler, Curator of the Royal Porcelain Museum at Worcester, has most kindly allowed the reproduction of the beautiful specimens of Worcester porcelain which adorn this book.

I must also thank Mr Bruce Bailey, Assistant Librarian of the Northampton College of Technology, for his work on the photographs and for drawing the marks in the reference list at the end.

CONTENTS

PREFACE   *Page* 13

1 Introduction   17

2 The Greater Firms   32

3 Other Firms: I   60

4 Other Firms: II   75

5 Pattern Numbers, Cyphers and Registration Marks   87

6 Conclusion   90

APPENDIXES

A Porcelain Artists of the Victorian Period   93

B Marks   98

C The Great Exhibition of 1851   105

D The Manufacture of Porcelain   113

E Glossary of Porcelain Terms   118

INDEX   123

ILLUSTRATIONS

BETWEEN PAGES 48-49

1 Pair of Minton pedestal vases painted by Thomas Allen

2 Pair of Minton vases with stands

3 Royal Crown Derby teaware with 'Mikado' pattern

4 Part of a Copeland and Garrett tea and coffee service

5 Chamberlain's Worcester plate in 'Imari' style

6 Booth's copy of Worcester 'Scale Blue and Birds' plate

7 Mason's two-handled ironstone vase in oriental style

8 Worcester vase in Japanese style

9 Worcester vase: pâte-sur-pâte on pink ground

10 Mason's ironstone vase in oriental style

11 Tall pâte-sur-pâte Minton vase by Solon

12 Worcester cake plate

13 Worcester saucer painted with flowers and ribbons

14 Chamberlain's Worcester plate

15 Rockingham plate: c. 1840

16 Crown Staffordshire covered vase in Chinese style

17 Vase, possibly Coalport, of 1842

18 Vase, possibly Rockingham: c. 1840

19 Davenport plate showing influence of Derby 'Imari' designs

20 Coalport plate in 'Rose Pompadour'

21 Worcester vase modelled by J. Hadley

22 Worcester vase in 'Ivory Porcelain' by J. Hadley

23 Worcester flower tube comport and plates

24 Worcester vase modelled by J. Hadley

25 Copeland vase decorated by C. F. Hürten

26 Worcester 'Parian' salt and inkwell by W. B. Kirk

27 Minton 'Parian' figure by John Bell

28 Copeland 'Parian' bust of Queen Victoria

29 Minton plaque painted by Daniel Lucas (possibly Copeland)

30 Worcester card tray: c. 1845

31 Two Copeland plates with painted views: c. 1830

32 Copeland plate with view of the Castle of Comares

BETWEEN PAGES 80–81

33 Copeland plate with a painting of the *Great Eastern*

34 Copeland plate painted by Arthur Perry with a view of Dinant

35 Minton teaware and coffee cup with saucer

36 Copeland tea set with matching tray

37 Pierced coupe shaped Minton plate by L. Boullemier

38 Copeland plate with the monogram of Queen Victoria

39 Minton vase with cover

40 Minton 'Ship' vase: probably by L. Boullemier

41 Belleek: mid-Victorian ice pail

42 Mid-Victorian Minton centre piece and vases

43 Centre pieces and a covered vase by Minton

44 Minton porcelain clock, thermometer and barometer

45 Copeland vases and ewer: mid-Victorian

46 Pair of Minton comports: mid-Victorian

47 Examples of mid-Victorian covered vases by Copeland

48 Group of mid-Victorian Minton vases

49 Four mid-Victorian Copeland vases

50 Worcester ewer and stand painted by Thomas Bott

51 Copeland plate of about 1840

52 Grainger's (Worcester) coffee service and toilet ware

53 'Great Porcelain Vase' exhibited at the Crystal Palace

Plates 1, 2 and 29 are reproduced by permission of the City Museum, Stoke-on-Trent, and 5, 6, 7, 10, 14, 15 and 51 by permission of the Northampton Museums Committee.

Nos. 11, 27, 35, 37, 38 and 39 are from the Works Museum of Mintons (11, 27, 35 and 37 appearing by the courtesy of *The Pottery Gazette and Glass Trade Review*), No. 3 is from the collection of the Royal Crown Derby Porcelain Company, and Nos. 4, 25, 28, 31, 32, 33, 34, and 36 are from the Museum of Messrs. Copeland.

Nos. 8, 9, 21, 22, 23, 24, 26 and 30 are from the collection of the Royal Porcelain Works at Worcester.

The drawings 41-52 are from Jewitt's 1878 edition of *Ceramic Art of Great Britain*.

PREFACE

IN THIS book I have kept roughly to the chronological limits of Victoria's reign, 1837–1901, but, since a number of the artistic ideas and designs of the period were adumbrated before it began and also persisted well into the Edwardian age that followed, I have not kept to these limits too strictly. Thus, although the Rockingham factory closed in 1842, and so only comes into the Victorian age at the very end of its career, its styles acted as an inspiration to later ceramic artists and therefore I have said almost as much about it as about some of the more specifically Victorian firms.

Again, both with the greater factories like Worcester and the small firms such as Booths or the Crown Staffordshire company, strong Victorian influences can be traced right up to at least 1914 and even later. It is indeed often difficult, and sometimes impossible, to be certain that what looks like a late Victorian piece may not in fact be Edwardian, and vice versa, unless there are incontrovertible marks which pin it down to particular years.

About the scope of this book: The term 'porcelain' has been very loosely used in the past and applied to many types of paste which are not porcelain in the true sense at all. Even the 1851 Exhibition Catalogue carried illustrations of gigantic 'porcelain vases', emanating from Russia, which, owing to their colossal size, can hardly have been of a truly porcellanous texture.

Many older books on ceramics also use the word 'china' in a vaguely defined way and compel it to cover various kinds of what is sometimes called 'semi-porcelain'.

However, as it was largely during the Victorian period that many of these ramifications of the older ceramic formulae were developed, I have not confined the scope of this handbook exclusively to 'true porcelain'. For this reason there will be found brief references to Ironstone China, 'Porcelaine Opaque', Silicon

China and one or two other types of paste which are either primarily or exclusively the result of Victorian experiments.

Parian ware is naturally included because it differs in texture from porcelain only in the proportion of its constituents and is therefore quite legitimately considered as a porcelain paste. It was also made in such vast quantities during the Victorian age that it cannot be neglected in any survey of the period's work. And in any case many beautiful specimens have survived, including some splendid Minton comports, with Parian figurines applied to the main body of the piece, which is itself of true porcelain.

The whole subject of Victorian porcelain is vast and complex, and perhaps no one book can hope to cover all its branches. The nearest approach to this was made in the Victorian age itself by Llewelyn Jewitt, whose monumental *Ceramic Art of Great Britain*, first published in 1878, gave detailed accounts of most of the important firms then practising. There were also accounts of the famous works of the past, some of which were, of course, even then long since defunct. Another important general book for the student is William Burton's *English Porcelain* (1902) which contains some interesting coloured plates, though many of Burton's opinions and criticisms may not commend themselves to the modern collector. Much which Burton lauded we now like less; on the other hand some of his strictures seem now far too severe since he was writing at the close of the Victorian age when it had acquired none of the patina of time which now gives it so much interest.

Burton had, however, a first-rate technical knowledge, and any collector specially interested in the technical details of porcelain manufacture should try to get a copy of his work.

There is also much of very great interest in Geoffrey Bemrose's *Nineteenth Century English Pottery and Porcelain* (1952).

Finally, all students and collectors of Victorian porcelain must be deeply indebted to Geoffrey Godden's scholarly work on the subject, published in 1961, which brought to light so much interesting material relating to the ceramic artists of the period. In this book I have adopted a different scheme from Mr Godden's and have said much more about the minor Victorian firms, including a number which he does not mention, together with some general advice for the collector and a short glossary of porcelain terms.

Conversely, I have said comparatively little about the porcelain artists themselves since reference should certainly be made to Mr Godden's book for detailed lists of all the principal artists attached to the greater firms.

Chapter One

Introduction

UNTIL recently the date 1830 was regularly used as a dividing line for the separation of 'genuine antiques' from the flood of later pieces which were not permitted to qualify for the title. The original idea behind the erecting of this severely preserved barrier seems to have been that anything produced before 1830 was inevitably of higher artistic quality than anything produced later, though there have always been connoisseurs of Victoriana who were unable to accept this distinction.

But with the growing interest in the finer achievements of the Victorian age this date-barrier is being more and more lifted, and perhaps nowhere is this more apparent than in the realm of porcelain. Old prejudices, however, still linger and die hard and this is why, apart from the enormous quantity of pieces produced during Victoria's long reign, it is still comparatively easy for the collector of modest means to find many delightful examples for his own cabinets. If he is not rich the porcelain of the great historical periods, Worcester under Dr Wall, Sèvres in the reign of Louis XV, or Meissen in the years of Kändler and Marcolini, will now be quite beyond his purse. But examples of Victorian porcelain are still, except for the choicest and most sumptuous specimens, well within the reach of anyone with a few pounds to spend. And though, with the rapidly growing interest in it, prices must inevitably rise, there is still much richly rewarding hunting to be done, especially at private house sales and the smaller provincial auction rooms where charming pieces may go at very reasonable figures.

Of course, the 1830 dividing-line was not erected in the first place solely by critics with an unrelenting prejudice against

Victoriana. There was much to justify such a barrier between 'antique' and 'non-antique', for after that date a vast tide of factory-made objects, not only in porcelain but in almost everything else, began to be loosed on the swarming new towns and suburbs of industrial England. A deterioration from the meticulously beautiful and loving standards of eighteenth-century hand craftsmanship (still preserved through the Regency period) set in almost at once. And by the time of the Great Exhibition of 1851 there had undoubtedly come a loss of refinement and a lack of balance which shows in many of the objects catalogued in the official list, though it has to be remembered that a number of them were definitely 'exhibition pieces' rather than things made for domestic use. However, much that was extremely fine and well worth the collector's attention was produced in Victorian times, and it is most unfortunate that we do not yet possess in England any comprehensive museum devoted exclusively to Victoriana where all branches of nineteenth-century art, including porcelain, could be studied.

Whether this will ever come cannot as yet be forecast, though with the constantly increasing interest in Victoriana it may well one day do so. In the meantime the student and collector can see some fine representative collections in different parts of the country, notably in London at the Victoria and Albert Museum, at Stoke-on-Trent in the Works Museums of Messrs Mintons and Copelands', and at the Hanley Museum and that of the Royal Porcelain Works at Worcester.

A number of dealers now specialize on Victoriana, including porcelain, and this in itself is evidence of the rapidly growing interest among collectors. And, although the porcelain of the time was produced in such vast quantities that the supply must last for a long time, the first-quality pieces are already in very heavy demand. The collector is therefore urged strongly to acquire any pieces of exceptional beauty which come his way since, if the supply is great, the demand is great also and seems likely to increase steeply as the more limited porcelain treasures of earlier periods grow increasingly out of reach.

The Victorians desired richness, elegance and comfort in their homes, and their porcelain, like their furniture, their wallpaper and their elaborate sweeping draperies, reflects most faithfully their essentially sumptuous decorative tastes. Modern ideas may often make their conception of 'elegance', whether in porcelain or anything else, difficult to appreciate; some of the pieces shown at the Great Exhibition of 1851, and at later displays, seem to us heavy and cumbrous, writhing with uncomfortable excesses of ill-planned ornament, and after the supreme standards of elegance of the eighteenth century a sad descent to the demands of the newly rich industrial *bourgeoisie* who were their principal patrons.

But in the eyes of the Victorians themselves all their principal decorative objects, whether chairs and sofas, candelabra and church ornaments, pottery and porcelain, were considered 'elegant', and the primary aim of their makers was to satisfy an increasing appetite for domestic comfort and splendour and to produce visible and tangible tokens of the vast new accumulation of wealth which was becoming available for thousands of English homes and public buildings.

The collector, in fact, before looking in detail at Victorian porcelain itself, might with advantage study a little the whole framework into which its elaborate and often quite magnificent pieces were designed to fit. And in addition to studying Victorian houses he might find it useful to take a preliminary glance at Victorian churches, theatres, town halls, museums, and even railway stations. For the porcelain of the period was really only a miniature branch of expression of that colossally self-confident and richly exuberant artistic temperament which gave us buildings like the Houses of Parliament, St Mary's Cathedral at Edinburgh, Covent Garden Opera House, Leeds Town Hall, the Museums of South Kensington, and St Pancras Station.

One thing will strike the collector very early if he makes this attempt to see Victorian porcelain as part of the general Victorian artistic scene. There is the same dominance of past ideals, the same strong historical sense which runs through the arts of the Victorian age as a whole, including painting and the drama as well as fiction, romantic poetry and architecture. He will notice at once, for instance, how influential was the wish to emulate the great historical porcelain achievements of Sèvres and Meissen in the eighteenth century. He may indeed quite soon in his collecting get the chance to acquire one of the splendid 'Rose Pompadour' plates produced by Coalport in imitation of those made by Sèvres nearly a century earlier, or a pair of Victorian candelabra in the style of Meissen in the Marcolini period.

And if he has learned to appreciate Victorian porcelain in the general setting of its age he will remember that this passion for emulating past styles was being pursued on the grand scale by Victorian millionaires like the Baron de Rothschild with his superb French-château style mansion at Waddesdon, and by the nation as a whole when it sponsored and financed the splendid Gothic palace of the Houses of Parliament.

But in recognizing this it is important at the outset to be fair to the Victorian artists and craftsmen, whether one is looking at one of their churches or houses, at a Victorian painting, or at a piece of Victorian porcelain. For at their best they usually produced something which had its own essential quality and was not simply a lifeless copy from the great ages of the past.

Anyone who looks without prejudice at, say, Millais' famous picture of the drowned Ophelia, or at some of the charming Tudor-style country railway stations along many English branch lines, or at a fine pair of Victorian Minton or Copeland vases, will have to admit that they have a strong character of their own. The models of the past have merely acted as a spur to the artists, not as a stranglehold crushing liveliness or adaptability to the needs of a fresh age.

As the nineteenth century went on, however, coarseness of detail and a frequent ugliness of conception become evident in all the decorative arts, reaching a climax in the 1860's and early 1870's after which the 'Aesthetic Rebellion', championed and popularized in the 1880's by Oscar Wilde and satirized by Gilbert in *Patience*, began to deal a series of blows at the cumbrous artistic fashions of the time.

Here again the collector, if he wishes to follow the progress of Victorian porcelain through its various phases from about 1830 to the end of the century, would gain much by studying the progress of artistic and cultural ideas as they developed towards the increasing refinement of the 1890's. For he will then see how, very gradually, the heaviness and coarseness of detail of the mid-century vanished from the artistic scene in all its branches. (Artistic history sometimes repeats itself, and in this gradual lightening of artistic touch during the later nineteenth century there is a strong parallel in France where the heavy formal grandeur of the styles of the Louis Quatorze era moved towards the more graceful asymmetry of the rococo period in the following century.)

For instance, in Victorian architecture it is interesting to trace the progress from the lumberingly solid Gothic of the churches and houses of the mid-century towards the lighter and more elegant 'Queen Anne' style of Norman Shaw and others. There was also the sudden wave of gracefulness produced by the cult of 'Japonaiserie', a fashion which reached popular expression in the theatre in *The Mikado* (1885) and a little later in *The Geisha* and other Japanese pieces. This cult of Japan is clearly reflected in the porcelain of the time with the growing popularity of Japanese designs with the greater firms. There was also, of course, an impetus to the collection of genuine Japanese examples and this in its turn exerted a fresh influence on the styles of the time.

Porcelain, then, viewed in this way, will be rapidly seen to be an integral part of the cultural stream of the Victorian age, not an isolated art developed by isolated ceramic artists in the great factories of Worcester and Derby and Stoke-on-Trent. It was a microcosm of contemporary taste, and an ability to visualize it against the setting for which it was designed and an insight into the culture of the age which produced it will make its collection infinitely more interesting, more authoritative and altogether better-informed.

But although Victorian porcelain faithfully reflects the tastes of its time in so many ways, especially in its suggestion of rich domestic comfort and commercial prosperity, in one respect it showed little contact with a most important source of contemporary inspiration—that of the Gothic Revival. For the Gothic influence, right through the Victorian period, was still a very potent influence-stimulus to the other arts, including architecture, poetry and painting. In architecture it produced a vast crop of pseudo-medieval buildings of all kinds, Gothic churches, Gothic colleges, Gothic breweries, Gothic lunatic asylums and even Gothic railway stations, many of which still stand.

In poetry the medieval influence is obvious in works like Tennyson's *Idylls of the King* and in Matthew Arnold's *Tristram and Iseult* and Swinburne's *Tristram of Lyonesse*. In painting there was the work of the pre-Raphaelites which also bore fruit in allied arts such as the making of stained-glass windows, large numbers of which can be seen adorning English churches to this day.

Porcelain, however, seems to have largely escaped the hand of the Goths, and for this we can, on the whole, feel profoundly thankful. However much the lover of the Victorian age finds himself drawn to the architecture of Pugin or Butterfield or Gilbert Scott, or to the canvases of Rossetti and Millais and Holman Hunt and Burne-Jones, it is not likely that he would feel much attracted to Gothic-style vases, teacups or dessert services.

From time to time, none the less, the collector will encounter occasional pieces, notably plates and vases, with delightful paintings suggestive of the medievalism of Sir Walter Scott, or Pugin and the Houses of Parliament.

I recently saw a very handsome set of plates and a covered bowl, clearly part of a former dinner-service, gorgeously gilded on a royal blue ground and with richly coloured paintings of scenes redolent of *Ivanhoe* and *Quentin Durward*—medieval castles, knights splendidly caparisoned, heraldic shields and banners glittering with crimson and gold, and all the panoply of Gothic Romance. Many a Victorian vase, too, will have its charming little melancholy landscape, often in soft tones of brown and green, with its cottage or ruined chapel, trees, distant mountains and foreground of lake or stream, the whole suggestive of that love of the romantic aspects of nature which was so strong a feature of the Gothic Revival.

Occasionally, too, Victorian vases will be found painted with heads of medieval or Tudor Kings and Queens, sometimes set in oval panels like those which Thomas Bott painted of Anne Boleyn and her father on the 'Ormond' vase produced by Worcester in the 1860's.

But these pieces were outside the main stream of influence on Victorian porcelain which was much more strongly governed by classical and Louis Quinze designs and standards, with, as we have seen, a strong admixture of Japanese influence later in the century. Of course, these classical and French trends can be discerned in architecture also, for along with the riot of Gothic pinnacles and turrets of so many buildings of the time there were many classical style erections, such as Leeds Town Hall, and dozens of theatres in which the prevailing influence was plainly that of the time of Louis Quinze. The cupids and 'Rose Pompadour' and heavy gilding of so much Victorian porcelain find their exact counterpart in many a Victorian dress-circle or theatre vestibule.

A full appreciation, therefore, of the achievements of the Victorian porcelain artists is dependent on a sympathetic understanding of their attitude to the styles of the past and their feeling that they were the continuators, not the mere copyists, of great traditions. We are coming now to a better realization of this in our judgements of the other arts of the nineteenth century and we should extend this to its porcelain too. We no longer think of, for instance, Garnier's Paris Opera House as a lifeless copy of Baroque, nor of Burne-Jones and the pre-Raphaelites as simply medieval copyists, nor of Swinburne's *Tristram of Lyonesse* as a piece of mock-Arthurian historicism.

Our own artistic canons have shifted so much in the direction of originality at all costs that we are apt to be, however, still sometimes too severe in our criticism of any form of art which drew strongly on the inspiration of the past and to brand it as merely derivative and reproductive. Occasionally, no doubt, this was so, but never in the hands of the best artists of the Victorian era.

Many of them, and well before the time of Morris's doctrines too, were men of progressive ideas intermingled with their artistic conservatism, and nowhere is this more apparent than in the best examples of the porcelain of the time.

Hideous things were undoubtedly produced (is the present age, however, in any position to cast stones in that direction?) and anyone with a taste for grotesquerie in his collecting might easily amass a special Cabinet of Horrors culled exclusively from the Victorian period. Terrifying vases encrusted with writhing nightmares of applied decoration, porcelain clock sets of abominable heaviness, ugly brown and black *jardinières*, ewers of pot-bellied proportions and china figures of an appalling flatness of face and limb together with animals of Jabberwockian dreadfulness—nothing, alas, would be easier to assemble than such a collection.

But just as Nature produces more specimens than can possibly survive, so the Victorian period, in the overwhelming rapidity of its growth, threw up vast quantities of objects which can never, however taste may revolve, have any commercial value for the collector and connoisseur. The important thing to remember always in collecting from the period is that one must be carefully selective; no other age produced such a wide differentiation of quality in its artistic examples.

ADVICE ON COLLECTING

Although Victoriana has advanced rapidly in favour during the last two or three decades there is still a vast amount of it available for the collector of modest means. House sales continue to yield great quantities of bric-à-brac, among which there is often much Victorian porcelain, and the stocks at auction rooms and dealers' shops seem unlikely to be diminished for some time to come.

But a great part of what one sees is of poor quality, badly painted and with inferior gilding, or, only too often, ugly and of coarse design. The sheer quantity of porcelain which was poured out during Victoria's reign makes its collection, even today, an *embarras de richesses* and frequently the riches may be said to be dangerously close to rags. For the selective collector and the selective dealer has for some time now been in search of the better specimens and it is not very probable that you will encounter many of the choicer pieces going cheaply.

Even so, it may safely be said that there are still more bargains to be had in Victoriana, including porcelain, than in any other branch of 'antiques for the modest collector', and if you are conveniently placed for hunts at market stalls and the smaller curio and antique shops, and able to attend house sales and the less frequented auction rooms in provincial towns, you are certain soon to be able to fill your cabinets with some delightful pieces.

I recently obtained from a market stall, and for only six shillings, three Victorian Worcester plates, in perfect condition, with the rare mark of the crowned W and the words 'Worcester Royal Porcelain Co. Works' which was only used for some eight years between 1862 and 1870. They are charming specimens, bordered with multi-coloured flowers and interlaced ribbons and, for any-one who wished to make a collection solely of Victorian Worcester they would be a decided and very inexpensive acquisition. Constant vigilance at market stalls and the smaller shops in my own district has, in fact, yielded to me a richly rewarding harvest of pleasant pieces, including specimens of Minton, Copeland, Davenport, Worcester, Coalport and Derby. I have also acquired many delightful unmarked examples, excellent blue and gold flower-painted vases, apple-green and gilded plates, several fine comports from Victorian dessert-services and a set of Booth's 'scale-blue and exotic birds' plates, all from the same market stall.

Collecting Victorian porcelain can be either general or of the work of particular firms, while a third kind of collecting could be of specimens of a particular genre, plates, teapots, vases, candelabra, tazzas, cups and saucers, Parian figures, ewers, centre-pieces, etc. Whichever kind you decide on (they can be easily combined if you wish) you will need a knowledge of makers' marks and at least an elementary understanding of the ways in which pieces can be dated, though this is not by any means always possible.

The collector of Victorian porcelain is fortunately spared one of the principal annoyances of antique collecting in general, at all events so far. He does not have to be constantly on his guard against forgeries and careful reproductions, for Victorian porcelain as a whole has not yet acquired sufficient commercial value to make its forgery a profitable business. No factory has yet begun to simulate Victorian vases along the lines of the 'gold anchor Chelsea' or 'old Sèvres' reproduction firms, though it may be only a matter of time and rising public demand before this happens. (Victorian-style glass paper-weights of the *millefiori* kind are already being manufactured and there are many modern reproductions of Victorian glass chandeliers.) As yet, however, apart from a few tourist souvenirs of the seaside pier and chain-store variety, Victorian porcelain presents a vast field of almost completely genuine examples, available in their hundreds and requiring only a carefully selective judgement and a relatively small outlay for the building of a collection.

But though it is unlikely that you will ever purchase anything as genuine Victorian which afterwards turns out to be spurious you may be deceived into thinking some of the Victorian reproductions of Sèvres and other kinds of antique porcelain are themselves genuine. On one famous occasion the directors of the Coalport firm were led to believe that one of their own vases was a piece of old Sèvres, so skilfully was it made. Obviously, when experts themselves can be so deluded the beginner cannot hope to escape an occasional pitfall. The Coalport 'Rose Pompadour' plates, for example, with gadrooned edges, raised gold decoration and reserves exquisitely painted with flowers are a remarkably faithful and beautiful reproduction of the spirit and technique of old Sèvres. And some of the Sèvres-style vases painted by Randall and others need the most careful examination to distinguish them from their great prototypes.

The collector, however, may decide that he would prefer to steer quite clear of all Victorian pieces which were merely imitative or reproductive, even if they were very brilliantly made. He may choose to concentrate entirely on specimens with their own unmistakable personality and flavour of the Victorian age, perhaps on collecting vases and plates where the figures and their settings are themselves a definite evocation of the period. Such a collection would certainly be of more historical interest than, for instance, an assembly of Victorian Sèvres-style vases, for reproductions can never be anything but reproductions and they usually capture little or nothing of the spirit of the age which made them.

Some of the vases produced by Coalport, for example, are painted with female heads and shoulders where the style of hairdressing and the costumes worn are essentially Victorian. Others, like those showing melancholy undraped ladies perched on rocks and strumming on harps while their hair streams romantically in the breeze, have also an unmistakable Victorian aura around them. They could never pass for pieces of old Sèvres or indeed for anything else than specimens of the 1850's and 1860's, and that, to many collectors, will be the essence of their charm.

It is difficult to say anything helpful to the collector about the prices he must expect to pay for Victorian porcelain since these fluctuate from time to time and from district to district, dependent on supply and demand. Good quality vases and plates suitable for wall decoration will always command a fairly high price, though charming single vases can sometimes be obtained for three or four pounds and pleasant plates at slightly less.

The better quality marked pieces will naturally fetch more than this, though I got a Coalport Rose Pompadour plate, with raised gold decoration and reserves of flowers, recently for only fifty shillings, and a delightful pair of tall two-handled vases in blue and gold with fine flower panels for five pounds, both pieces being in perfect condition. These tended, however, to be exceptional bargains; normally one would have to pay more for similar specimens, and I have seen vases not very different from these priced at thirty or forty pounds and even more.

But certainly no one need be deterred from collecting Victorian porcelain on the grounds of cost. There is more available in the lower-priced category than in any other branch of porcelain, and if you are looking merely for single specimens, such as comports that have become isolated from their original dessert-services, or for single plates, cups and saucers, vases, etc., you can still build up a collection at a very reasonable outlay.

Much the most satisfactory way of collecting is by constant personal attendance at house and auction-room sales where the collector will soon learn for himself what prices are being reached in his own area and bid accordingly. But a number of antique dealers now carry good stocks of Victorian porcelain and excellent pieces can often be got from them at reasonable figures. If a dealer knows that you have an interest in building up a collection he may often be able to get for you specimens you could not acquire yourself without his professional contacts.

Many forms of specialized collecting are possible with Victorian porcelain, quite apart from the collecting of specimens of particular firms such as Worcester or Coalport. For instance, a most interesting assembly could be made of objects illustrating the 'Japonaiserie' cult of the later nineteenth century and its influence on contemporary porcelain. Special collections could be made of various porcelain fashions of the period, such as the 'jewelled' ware of Worcester and other firms, of the work of particular painters (though these are often hard to identify), or of bird and flower painting of the period. A collection showing French influence on the porcelain of the time could yield a very splendid assembly, with Minton and Coalport examples perhaps predominant, though many other firms produced excellent work in the style of Sèvres. Again, collections of particular articles, vases, porcelain clocks, figures and so on could well be made, or of pieces illustrating various processes, such as the famous Minton acid gold process, or the way in which individual colourings, such as Sardinian green, Rose Pompadour, turquoise or Bleu-du-roi were developed at the different factories.

DAMAGE AND REPAIRS

In the more lavish days of antique collecting, when it was much easier to acquire first-class pieces of all kinds than now, collectors were always strongly advised never to buy anything that was not in absolutely flawless condition. But antiques, particularly porcelain, are collected by far greater numbers of people than formerly, and the obtaining of completely perfect examples at reasonable prices is getting more and more difficult. Porcelain is by its very nature especially liable to damage, and the cloud which hung over the arts of the Victorian age for so long meant that many lovely pieces of its china were treated with scant respect, often being bundled clumsily into cupboards and either forgotten or despised.

As a result damage has often occurred, and scores of interesting pieces will come up before the collector at auction rooms and house sales which have suffered either minor or major ill-treatment. He will then often find himself wondering whether to purchase or not, since money values have to be considered even by the most ardently interested student, and if he wishes to sell the pieces again it will not be easy to dispose of them. The best general advice that can be given is that, if the damage is only slight and does not interfere with the general appearance of the piece, and if the specimen is of genuine interest (for instance, a Worcester plate with one of the rarer Victorian marks) then by all means buy it, though not at a high price. On the whole it is better to buy vases and centre-pieces with slight damage than plates or cups since often they can be so placed that a slight flaw or crack can be concealed, whereas with a damaged plate or cup it is virtually impossible to hide the fault. And when the damage to a vase is confined to its rim, as it quite often is, flowers or foliage placed inside will usually cover it up.

As for the repair of damaged pieces, it cannot be too strongly emphasized that the repair of porcelain is not to be lightly undertaken by amateurs, and it is always best to put the work out to a firm of professional restorers. For unless the collector is himself a skilled artist he will find it difficult, and often impossible, to match the colourings of antique porcelain with modern paints, to say nothing of the great professional skill required in repairing any damage to the paintings on the piece. If the damage is confined to something very simple, such as a gold rim or the extreme tip of a handle which can be remodelled with plastic wood or one of the very good china mending pastes now available, then you may perhaps essay the repair yourself. Even so, it is wise to get some practice first, on cheap or unwanted pieces, before starting on anything valuable.

Regilding, too, is apt to be much more difficult than it looks, since the variety of shades of gold used in the past is remarkable, and it is not easy to match the various lovely mellow golds to which time may have added its own inimitable patina.

You can, however, often buy up, from market stalls and the smaller antique shops, suitable vase lids and covers, which can be stored if not immediately needed, for use in connection with slightly imperfect pieces. Very often a beautiful vase may come your way, either lacking its original cover or damaged in a slight way which the addition of a cover would completely conceal. By having your odd covers either professionally gilded or repainted in some ground colour to match your damaged vases you can then often make a very satisfactory concealment of the faults.

If you are a complete perfectionist you will not, of course, in any event want to purchase any damaged pieces, however beautiful. But it is surprising how often really interesting and rare specimens appear at sales with merely some very slight flaw or fracture, and since so much might be learned from them if they were in your collection it may well be stretching perfectionism too far to reject them outright. You will almost invariably see professional dealers at sales turning away at once at the first sight of anything that is not in flawless condition and some collectors tend to catch this habit too readily themselves. But remember that the dealer is primarily interested in everything with a view to making a profit, and he knows from experience that the sale of even slightly damaged porcelain is going to be difficult. He may not want the expense and delay of putting the pieces out to a firm of restorers, but the collector is not faced with the same problems and can consequently cast his net far wider. He may, too, often encounter a fine pair of vases of which only one is perfect. Here again the dealer will have to eschew such pieces since it is unlikely that he can sell the single perfect vase at a figure that will recoup his outlay on the pair.

But the collector, who is merely anxious to add a fine specimen to his collection, can safely buy the two vases and either put the damaged one out to be repaired, or, if it has gone beyond all ceramic surgery, simply discard it.

Finally, if you decide to have any of your specimens professionally repaired (and happy indeed is the collector who never has an accident in his own home, even if he himself never purchases anything which is damaged) you well may find you will have to wait some time before getting your pieces returned. The first-class china restorers are kept constantly busy with a stream of intricate, delicate and very laborious work which cannot possibly be hurried, and whatever you send to them will have to wait its turn which may be several months or even a year in coming. A little amateur practice on your own will soon convince you of the necessity for extreme care, endless patience and meticulous professional skill in the restoration of broken porcelain, and time is of the very essence of the procedure.

Also, restoration is expensive, and again if you try a little yourself you will rapidly see why. Even the smallest chip off a piece may require several hours of most careful work to replace it satisfactorily; if it is a major breakage, involving perhaps the repainting of several flowers or exotic birds, or a complex piece of regilding, it may need several days and even weeks of careful thought and work before it can be pronounced perfect again.

Damage to porcelain, in fact, is always a disaster which it is an expensive and difficult business to put right. This is the principal reason why absolutely perfect specimens are invariably so much higher priced than anything with only the smallest flaw. I recently had to pay more than twice as much for a perfect apple-green and gold plate as for its exact fellow on which there were several very slight and hardly perceptible scratches, and at the time it seemed an unfair differentiation. But the repair of those scratches has been an expensive matter, involving a considerable wait, and clearly the perfect plate was, in the long run, well worth the extra cost.

Chapter Two

The Greater Firms

MINTON

THE manufacture of porcelain has never been so much centralized in England as in some other countries, but the metropolis of it has for a very long period been at Stoke-on-Trent, although other famous works, such as Worcester and Derby, have developed in different areas.

Prominent among the greater firms of Stoke, and specially distinguished during the nineteenth century, was the Minton factory whose history goes back to 1793. It was the Victorian period which witnessed the firm's greatest efflorescence and, with their notable development of the *pâte-sur-pâte* technique under Solon, their most famous contribution to ceramic history, but the pre-Victorian years at Mintons had already given more than a foretaste of the splendours shortly to come.

Several highly skilled workers from Derby had joined the firm, including Steele, Bancroft and Hancock, all notable painters of fruit and flowers, and when, on the death of Thomas Minton, the founder of the firm, in 1836, his son Herbert Minton assumed control, he inaugurated a period of ceramic experiments which were to make the name of Minton one of the most lustrous in the entire field of Victorian porcelain.

A number of celebrated French porcelain artists were soon attracted to Mintons, beginning with Léon Arnoux who began work with them in 1849. Arnoux supervised the manufacture of an entirely new porcelain body, made from Cornish and Dorsetshire clay worked into a cream and subjected to different degrees of heat in the firing than was customary at the time. Owing to the technical difficulties involved this had to be abandoned, but

Arnoux stayed on as artistic director and was only the first of a long series of brilliant French designers which included Carrier de Belleuse, afterwards a Commissioner at Sèvres, Anton Boullemier and the most famous of all, M. L. Solon. It was the last named who brought permanent fame to the firm as the developers of the *pâte-sur-pâte* process in which liquid clay applied to the body of the piece in the form of the design required produced decoration with a cameo-like effect, standing out from its background and yet being an integral part of it.

By 1851 Mintons had already achieved the highest repute and had presented at the Crystal Palace, among other fine quality specimens, a superb dessert-service which was purchased by Queen Victoria from the exhibition stand. This included oval and triangular baskets, wine coolers, elevated and low comports, cream bowls, jelly stands and salt cellars and *assiettes montées*.

Many other magnificent works were also shown and strong French influences were already apparent, as in the 'pair of candlesticks with figures in the costume of the time of Louis XV' and the 'inkstand, Sèvres green cross-bars, painted wreaths of flowers, and gilt'. French influence, in fact, can be discerned at Mintons during the whole of the Victorian period, but the firm was always progressive and was never content merely to copy slavishly the famous masterpieces of antique French porcelain. Thus, when, in 1870, Solon joined the works, having left Paris at the time of the Franco-Prussian War, he brought with him from Sèvres a wide knowledge of French methods of porcelain manufacture, but from the first he was encouraged to experiment extensively. The result of his stay at Mintons was the evolution of a technique and style which were highly individual and not a mere adaptation of the methods of Sèvres to English manufacture.

The *pâte-sur-pâte* technique, which is now so inseparably connected with Solon's name, had been, however, evolved at Sèvres where it was known as *pâte rapportée* and also as *pâte d'application*. But Solon gave it completely fresh individuality and wrote interesting accounts of his methods and life at Mintons which throw light on his genuine originality as an artist as well as

c

his astonishing technical skill. He describes how his development of *pâte-sur-pâte* differed from other methods of raised decoration and shows how much personal artistic skill was required for its success. He distinguishes between it and the method of making white reliefs on Wedgwood jasper ware, where each part of the model is pressed on a plaster mould and then stuck on to the body of the piece. Any number of copies may be produced by this process which simply requires careful workmanship for successful results.

Pâte-sur-pâte, however, where the decoration is made an integral part of the porcelain, can only be carried out by the artists themselves; no mechanical repetition is possible since each piece of decoration has to be individually moulded.

The type of paste in use at Mintons during the late Victorian period was much superior for the *pâte-sur-pâte* process to those employed in France and Germany, where only a few metallic oxides (essential for colouring the porcelain) could be used owing to the high degree of heat necessary in the firing. Mintons were able to increase the scale of colours very considerably, since they employed a form of felspathic paste where the elements were in different proportion from the normal hard porcelain formula.

Solon also makes it clear that Wedgwood jasper ware was not even the inspiration behind his *pâte-sur-pâte* technique; it evolved from a Chinese celadon vase at the Sèvres Museum, and he gives a most valuable account of his methods of procedure, which were simple enough for him to suggest that other artists, and even amateurs, might care to try their hand at it:

A vase of unbaked clay, which can be of various colours such as celadon or sage green, is passed through a muffle-kiln when it will, of course, both harden and contract by about one seventh of its original size. Unbaked clay, usually white or delicately tinted, is then laid on to the vase diluted with water into the consistency of batter ('slip' is the technical name for this) and applied in thin washes with a brush in the form of the decoration desired. The washes are continued until the necessary thickness is obtained, each wash being carefully allowed to dry before the next is put on.

This is the entire process, the rest depending 'more on the artistic feeling of the operator than on professional secrets.'

Authenticated pieces by Solon are now worth large sums of money since each was an individual creation of great delicacy and beauty. At Sotheby's in 1965 one of his most famous vases, an amphora painted in white slip and decorated with a frieze of Spartan girls wrestling before Lycurgus, realized £2,250. (This however, had even in 1903 sold for 1,500 guineas so that the valuation placed on it then was in fact higher than that of today, considering the change in the value of money.)

Of the many other wonderful achievements of Solon mention may be made of two remarkable examples of his technical virtuosity, 'The Vintage' and 'The Siren'. The first shows a classical-style harvest scene, with children pressing grapes, to which surrounding female figures bring baskets of fruits while overhanging foliage of incredible lightness and grace forms an elaborate framework to the scene. 'The Siren' is a splendidly shaped two-handled vase on which a winged mermaid-like figure plays a harp, the whole set against a background of foliage and branches again managed with consummate technical skill.

Solon seems to have had no feelings of false modesty, and his pupils and assistants were seldom allowed to take credit for their own work by signing their pieces. His artistic integrity, however, was undeniable and if any collector can now add a genuine Solon specimen to his cabinet he will have made an acquisition certain to rise in value as the finer achievements of Victorian porcelain increase in general esteem. His greater vases are infinitely more wonderful to see in reality than illustrations might lead one to suppose; certainly nothing at the splendid Minton Works Museum impressed me more than the magnificent assembly of these superb individual creations.

Solon's name has come to be regarded as the greatest in Mintons' history during the Victorian period, but many other fine artists achieved distinction there also. Carrier de Belleuse, for example, produced some very beautiful Parian figures such as 'Autumn', a graceful and very French female who perhaps looks as though she would be more at home in the Galerie des Glaces at Versailles than in a cornfield but is none the less a fine piece of work. Protât, a well-known sculptor who afterwards designed some of the statues at the India Office, also worked for Mintons; painters of distinction included Lessore, originally at Sèvres and subsequently famous at Wedgwoods, Boullemier, Jahn, Henk, Mussill and the Englishman, Thomas Allen, celebrated as a painter of figures.

Boullemier had painted porcelain at Sèvres as well as at several other Parisian factories, and his work for Mintons included many delightful Cupid and figure studies. He was a notable personality in the Stoke area, having musical talents as well as being a fine painter; he had refused a professional career at the Opéra Comique in Paris in order to continue with his painting of porcelain, and he was long remembered in the district for his organization of musical events. He seems to have been a character for Arnold Bennett.

Of the other artists mentioned, Thomas Allen was specially notable and some of his Sèvres-style vases are among the most beautiful pieces produced by the firm during the entire nineteenth century. He was an excellent figure-painter, though he also painted flowers, and his work was shown in various international exhibitions, including the Crystal Palace and the Exhibition of 1862. The grace and charm of his cupids and groups in the manner of Sèvres were almost worthy of their great prototypes of the eighteenth century and, though little of his work was signed, if the collector could acquire specimens of Allen's work they would, apart from their intrinsic beauty, be well worth buying as an investment since his reputation has always been high and is likely to be enhanced as time goes on.

William Mussill was yet another artist who had worked at Sèvres before joining Mintons and his brilliantly coloured flower paintings were remarkable for their fidelity to nature; he made many original drawings from conservatory specimens before putting his designs on porcelain. He was also a fine bird painter.

Other Minton artists worthy of note were Edmond Reuter,

Herbert Foster, and Albert Wright. Reuter had studied flower painting in Paris and was himself a botanist's son; Foster was especially versatile, celebrated for his figure paintings of contemporary celebrities as well as for his animal and bird designs; Wright also painted birds in a style full of delicate charm, though he painted floral and scenic subjects as well.

Henk was another painter who produced some very splendid vases in the manner of Sèvres, but they are essentially derivative in style and no doubt their aim was simply to recreate for the homes of the wealthier Victorian *bourgeois* patron the pink and gold atmosphere and *bleu-du-roi* splendours of porcelain of the Pompadour era, with cupids *à la* Boucher and elegant ladies and gentlemen *à la* Watteau.

The famous colourings of old Sèvres were reproduced at Mintons with astonishing skill, including the turquoise, Rose Pompadour (usually called 'Rose du Barri'), pea green and *gros bleu*, and actual Sèvres pieces, such as the famous 'Vaisseau à mat' in the Wallace Collection, were copied with wonderful technical ability.

It has been objected that many of the pieces produced by the above-mentioned artists were too richly covered and that they failed to observe that important principle of porcelain decoration whereby some of the porcelain is left in its natural state. But reticence was never a characteristic of the Victorians in anything they attempted. Certainly no one who wants reticence is likely to be attracted to Victorian porcelain any more than to Victorian architecture, Victorian painting, or Victorian poetry.

Under the energetic direction of Herbert Minton the firm widely expanded its activities and during the mid nineteenth century added some important technical developments to their programme. These included their famous 'Acid Gold' process, for which Letters Patent were granted in 1863. The actual invention of this was the work of James Leigh Hughes, but the patent rights were soon acquired by Mintons and the term 'acid gold' came to be indissolubly connected with their name, the process being in fact still in use. A bas-relief pattern in gold is obtained through hand engraving of the design on copper, the pattern then being transferred to tissue paper and subsequently applied to the china as a black design. The articles are then dipped in a bath of hydrofluoric acid, the whole surface, except for the pattern, being protected against the action of the acid which turns the black design to a pattern resembling white lace. Two coats of gold are then given to the pattern, and after the raised portions of the design are burnished the sunk portions are left in the matt gold state.

This very beautiful result has made the acid gold process a favourite for services which include coats of arms or monograms, and has led to innumerable special orders from royalty and governmental bodies in all parts of the world for over a hundred years.

An interesting off-shoot of the Minton works in Victorian times was the development of the manufacture of encaustic tiles, a department which from small beginnings, grew to enormous dimensions. This venture, afterwards known as Minton, Hollins and Co. and based at 'The Patent Tile Works, Stoke-on-Trent' numbered among its very first patrons the architect Pugin who used Minton tiles in the decoration of the new Houses of Parliament. Subsequently a vast business developed in the making of glazed tiles for many purposes, such as wall decoration, flower-boxes, fireplaces, church floors, reredoses, etc. At the Philadelphia Exhibition of 1876 much interest was attracted by a complete chimney-piece executed entirely in ornamental tiles in a geometrical design alternating with brilliantly painted humming birds, the whole surrounding an elaborate picture composed of thirty tiles depicting a mother and her children.

(Occasionally separate specimens of Minton tiles can be picked up at sales. I got one recently showing 'Abraham offering up his son Isaac', a somewhat terrifying composition in black and white, complete with sacrificial brazier, knife dramatically poised in Abraham's hand, and the ram caught in a thicket discreetly placed on one side. It is in perfect condition and gives the impression of having never been used; it may have been a sample for a scheme of church decoration.)

Some idea of the world-wide fame achieved by Minton during the Victorian era may be gained by a mere list of the international awards they obtained from 1851 onwards. Beginning with the Crystal Palace, they received 'firsts' at Paris in 1853, 1867, and 1878, again in London in 1862, at Moscow in 1872, Vienna 1873, Philadelphia 1876, Melbourne 1881, and Calcutta 1884.

The great firm is still in full operation and producing magnificent work and certainly its fine Victorian pieces are likely to be in ever increasing demand among collectors as time goes on. Anyone who wishes to make a collection of Victorian porcelain could have a superb assemblage simply on Minton pieces alone.

COPELAND

Among the great Victorian manufactories of England none had a more distinguished record than that of the Copeland works, Copelands being the successors of the famous firm of Spode. Alderman W. T. Copeland, who afterwards became Lord Mayor of London, acquired the business of the third Josiah Spode in 1833 and with his partner and senior traveller, Thomas Garrett, continued the firm under the style of 'Copeland and Garrett' until 1847. The partnership was then dissolved and the name changed to 'W. T. Copeland late Spode', becoming in 1867 'W. T. Copeland and Sons'.

Perhaps the most notable contribution to ceramic history made by the Copeland firm was the development of Parian ware, a purely Victorian achievement which, however, had its origins in the earlier Derby biscuit ware, some of whose moulds and models were acquired by Alderman Copeland.

There is some doubt about the actual invention of Parian for, although Copelands were certainly the first firm to produce it in large quantities, Messrs T. and R. Boote may have been the actual originators of the material in the early 1840's. This company was always interested in progressive ideas and in 1843 they took out a patent for 'certain improvements in pottery and mosaic work' and again in 1857 for 'improvements in the manufacture of ornamental pottery and articles made from clay and other like plastic materials'. They definitely produced Parian pieces very early in the history of the material and by 1851 were exhibiting fully developed Parian work at the Crystal Palace. Among their various later Parian pieces was an elaborate religious group entitled 'Repentance, Faith and Resignation', by Gillard, which seems to breathe the very spirit of Victorian piety and must have provided many a moment of moral uplift in whatever Victorian rectory or household it found a home. The three figures, in attitudes of meek submission, are grouped around a cross, their heads bent, their eyes suitably downcast and their whole attitudes symbolical of 'calm of mind, all passion spent'. It would be hard to find another group of figures so thoroughly imbued with the religious sentiments of the time.

Copelands, however, were certainly very active in the early development of Parian, for shortly after 1840 a worker from the Derby factory joined the Copeland and Garrett works and was encouraged to make experiments to revive the lost art of Derby biscuit figure-making, which had produced such beautiful results in the eighteenth century, and was at that time highly admired. A proportion of felspar had been used in the making of Spode's china, and in the experiments made at Copelands this was again employed; eventually the marble-like body known as Parian was evolved. This form of paste, which derives its name from its resemblance to Parian marble, was composed of a mixture of the same ingredients as true porcelain, but in a different ratio, the fusible and infusible elements being usually in the proportion of two to one instead of in equal quantities.

The Derby worker, Mountford, subsequently claimed the credit for this valuable invention, but it was also claimed by Garrett himself and by Battam, the art director at Copelands at the time. The likelihood is that all three had a part in it so that it was, in fact, a joint invention to which each individual thought he had contributed the lion's share.

Parian has not the waxen quality of the old Derby biscuit porcelain, but its close resemblance to marble made it of great commercial value to Copelands and for many years they produced large quantities of Parian figures and groups, many of which must survive in various parts of the world. After a time, however, public appetite for Parian was sated and it ceased to be fashionable, but other firms took up the manufacture of it, notably Worcester (both the Royal Porcelain Works and Grainger's) where 'pierced Parian' vases of very high quality and astonishing dexterity were produced.

In addition to Parian ware Copelands became famous during the Victorian period for their splendid dinner- and tea-services while one of the most sumptuous achievements in their entire history was the famous dessert-service made for the Prince of Wales in 1866. Its 198 pieces, all individually designed, included 72 cups and saucers, 50 plates, and a magnificent centre-piece with a decoration of orange-blossom, in compliment to the Prince's marriage, as a prominent motif in the floral painting. Finely modelled figures, representative of the four quarters of the earth, the months of the year and the elements, adorned the centre-piece and the fruit dishes, with flower panels embellished with raised gold decoration and incorporating the monogram of the Prince and his bride.

Copelands also produced some exquisite new colourings for their porcelain, their 'cerulean blue' and 'Sardinian green' attracting much contemporary admiration, as did their *bleu du roi*, their vermilion (notably used in the celebrated Mecklenburg service exhibited in 1889), and the so-called 'Rose du Barri'.

They were, too, among the most successful of Victorian manufacturers in the adaptation of Japanese ideas to English porcelain, their 'Satsuma' ware being characterized by a specially fine glaze, while in other designs they sometimes successfully combined English and Japanese motifs on the same piece.

Painted and enamelled tiles for mural decoration were another speciality of Copelands, and one of their most brilliant achievements was a decorative scheme which they carried out in the mid-Victorian period for a private mansion in Glasgow. With characteristic Victorian energy whole rooms of this extraordinary house were covered with celadon tiles, carefully manufactured to be completely damp-resistant and all adapted to the purposes of the various rooms. In the billiard room, for instance, there was a complete mural Panorama of Sport, each wall representing some admired aspect of the British character with its appropriate pastime, Health on one wall, Strength on another, Courage on the third, and Fortitude on the fourth. 'Courage' depicted not only British sports but those of the Oriental and American colonies, together with scenes of Shipwreck and Fire, a true piece of Victorian exuberance with a strong flavour of contemporary melodrama.

The Great Exhibition of 1851 acted as a superb national and international show-window for English porcelain, and no firm took better advantage of it than Copelands. From then on the firm went from strength to strength, culminating in their triumphs at the Paris Exhibition of 1889 where, among many other exhibits, their famous 'Midsummer Night's Dream' dessert-service attracted widespread admiration. The centre-piece depicted Titania asleep, under a canopy of branches and encircled by foxglove and some of the other flowers mentioned by Shakespeare. Eight tall comports, in the form of tree-stems and covered with trailing and climbing plants, and each adorned with a charming fairy figure, were supplemented by numerous smaller comports supported by pixies and elves.

It was at this Exhibition too that the celebrated reproduction of the old Chelsea dinner-service in the possession of the Grand Duchess of Mecklenburg-Strelitz won fresh admiration for the Copeland modellers and painters.

The great variety of the Copeland products is noteworthy and helps to explain why so many of their designs have come down to us today. Vases, tazzas, bottles, fireplace-panels, jugs, brackets and flower-stands, as well as a vast quantity of dinner and dessert-services, were manufactured by the firm in a wealth of different styles of decoration, painted, jewelled, enamelled, gilded, and adorned with alto-relievo figures and flowers. Slabs and plaques, finely painted with roses, chrysanthemums, begonias and azaleas, vases 'in the Moorish taste', plates with paintings after Angelica Kauffmann, oviform vases, vases 'grounded in Lincoln green enriched with gold', panels with cupids in the style of Boucher, dessert-services painted with English flowers—these, and innumerable other works combined to win for Copelands their tremendous prestige in the Victorian era, with its climax of the Grand Prix at Paris in 1889.

The best known artists at Copelands during the Victorian period were Hürten, famous as one of the finest contemporary flower painters in the whole of Europe, Weaver, a most distinguished bird painter, Besche, well known for his figure painting, and Abraham, who with his son also produced some fine figure painting.

Perhaps Copelands flower paintings are their most charming achievement for they have a peculiar charm of colour and a delightful lavish tenderness of expression which the collector soon learns to distinguish and appraise, though it is impossible to put into words the exact quality they seem to exude. The splendid flowers of Spode appear to be hovering like stimulating ghosts behind the Copeland roses and chrysanthemums, and possibly this is the real essence of their charm. I have, for instance, a pair of Victorian Copeland cups and saucers on which delicate groups of roses, pink, yellow and deep red, alternate with single blooms on a white ground, the border being in dark blue patterned with gold. The pieces seem to breathe the air of Spode, their great ancestor, and yet they have their own unmistakable freshness and personal character, and in this they are truly representative of the best Victorian art, at once respecting the great traditions of the past and yet clearly expressive of the age from which they sprang.

COALPORT

The Victorian achievements of Coalport are dominated by their magnificent reproductive work in the style of Sèvres, and if this resulted in less originality than was evident with some other firms, such as Mintons, the splendour of the Coalport pieces must be their justification.

When the Victorian era opened John Rose, who had raised Coalport to a position of the highest eminence in English porcelain, was still alive. He died, however, in 1841, and was succeeded by his nephew William, who presided at Coalport for a dozen years. William Rose was responsible for the inauguration of the famous 'Rose Pompadour' tint which caused so much interest at the Great Exhibition of 1851, when the firm displayed the fine dessert-service afterwards bought by Lord Ashburton. At that time the tint was generally known as 'Rose du Barry' (sometimes spelt 'Barri'), but it ultimately reverted to its proper title, 'Rose Pompadour'; the colour was, of course, first used at Sèvres many years before Mme. du Barry's reign. The term 'Rose du Barry', however, remained in use for many years in various circles; descriptions of theatrical decoration right up to the last quarter of the nineteenth century still sometimes used it.

The Crystal Palace Catalogue helped to foster the misnomer in its description of the Coalport pieces: 'In these services is shown an attempt at the revival of the beautiful pink or rose colour found on the old *pâte tendre* of Sèvres, known as the Rose du Barry. Madame Dubarry having some vases executed at the Sèvres works, the rose colour was adopted, as being the lady's favourite, in compliment to her. Colours of this character are usually produced by combinations of gold with salts of ammonia, to which sometimes tin and the oxide of manganese are added.'

The success of the 1851 exhibits amounted to a triumph for Coalport and was instrumental in launching the firm on a large-scale production of sumptuous pieces in the manner of Sèvres. Confidence in the accuracy of their reproductions was such that they even used the Sèvres mark of the interlaced L's, and when copies of old Chelsea vases were also made the gold anchor mark was put on too.

The best known artists working at Coalport on these splendid pieces were Randall, whose bird paintings were of an exquisite beauty almost worthy of the great days of Aloncle and Noel at

Sèvres, Cook, famous for flowers, and Hartshorne, who specialized on animals. Attempts were made by the later proprietors, the Bruffs (who bought the business on the death of William Pugh, Rose's partner), to introduce a fresher note into the designs and to avoid all direct imitation of the earlier Sèvres models. A period of stagnation had undoubtedly set in at Coalport in the 1860's and early 1870's, and it was only owing to the energy of the Bruffs, who reorganized the works with great thoroughness, that the firm was able to forge ahead and win fresh distinction in the latter years of the century.

Among other reforms the Bruffs decided to revive some of the old Chinese designs which had made Coalport famous in the past, the most popular being the ubiquitous willow pattern and the Broseley blue dragon design.

The work of Coalport during the Victorian era, if one views it as a whole, was not by any means of uniform excellence, either of design or of execution. It shared to the full in the outbreak of ugly forms and crude elaboration which were such marked features of so many of the 'art products' of the 1851 Exhibition, and examples of this are unfortunately only too easy to find. Some of its vases, covered, or should one say smothered with 'applied flowers', on shapes that are top-heavy, with wildly debased rococo handles and with covers set on them like hats that do not fit, give the impression of having emerged from the kiln distorted through having had their firing-contraction imperfectly allowed for. On other pieces the designs are inartistic, and even some of the Sèvres-style Rose Pompadour plates are spoiled by awkward panelling and injudicious spacing of the rose ground against the white porcelain of the plate itself.

A quite disastrous piece of design was that of the plates in the dessert-service made for Queen Victoria herself as a presentation set to the Tsar Nicholas I of Russia. Commissioned in 1845 through A. B. and R. P. Daniell, the Bond St and Wigmore St dealers, it appeared with the other Coalport exhibits at the Crystal Palace in 1851. It displayed the different orders of the Russian Empire tastelessly enamelled in reserves and surrounded by a border of Mazarine blue, heavily gilded and with very badly shaped gadrooned edges. For ponderous ugliness its design would be hard to beat, and it was the fact that such work could be commissioned even for important patrons that tended to give the Victorian age a bad name among connoisseurs of porcelain, and to obscure the very real charm of its more delightful examples.

Coalport also, as has been mentioned, was not scrupulous about putting forged Sèvres and Chelsea marks on its reproductions during the Victorian era. Perhaps, though, at this distance of time we may view this with the same tolerance that we now extend to the Chinese potters' 'earlier reign' marks as indicating simply that the pieces were in that style. And, of course, no collector, once he is passed the novice stage, is likely to imagine that the late Victorian Coalport pieces stamped 'Coalport A.D. 1750' were actual pieces of that date. It was merely the foundation date of the parent firm, though it might have saved some misconceptions by the unwary if the firm had made this more clear.

Many technical experiments were made by the Victorian porcelain manufacturers, but even in pre-Victorian days there was a good deal of experimental work going on, especially at Coalport where Rose was engaged in 1820 on the production of a new glaze which was to be free from the injurious effects of lead on the health of the workers. Eventually this was successfully made, and Rose was awarded a Gold Medal by the Society of Arts for his efforts. The constituents of the new glaze were felspar with a large proportion of borax, together with silicate of soda and potash, the whole fusing at a comparatively low temperature. This easily fusible quality meant that the enamelled colourings sank readily into the glaze during the firing and produced an effect quite as satisfactory as that of the dangerous lead formula.

Rose also at about the same time introduced pure felspar into his porcelain paste, the result being known as Coalport Improved Felspar Porcelain. It has been suggested that these great technical successes spurred him on to his ambitious emulation of the work of Sèvres and Chelsea and even to imitate their marks as a sign of his confidence. Many of the later Coalport imitations of Sèvres, however, are completely unmarked, including some of the Rose Pompadour and raised gold dinner plates, single specimens of which can still be found in the antique shops from time to time. (In 1855 one of these Sèvres-style services was actually purchased by the French Emperor, a remarkable compliment to the skill of the Coalport artists.)

In addition to the Rose Pompadour colour, which contemporary critics so much admired, Coalport also introduced a rich 'Sardinian green'. This was successfully used on many pieces, including wine-goblets, with raised and jewelled gold borders, flowers in 'tablets', and paintings of birds.

A fine purplish blue was also used as a ground for 'Japan' patterns when the fashion for things Japanese began to invade English ceramic decoration.

WORCESTER

Worcester is perhaps the most distinguished of all names in the history of English porcelain, for no other firm has such a long and unbroken record of excellence. When the Victorian period opened Worcester already had a famous past; its glories under Dr Wall had given it European fame, and early specimens were even then being carefully collected and preserved.

The history of its ownership dates from 1751 and is of great complexity, and at the beginning of the Victorian era there were three separate porcelain manufactories within the city of Worcester, those of Flight, Barr and Barr, Chamberlain and Co., and the Grainger works, run by Humphrey Chamberlain. In 1840, however, Flight, Barr and Barr amalgamated with Chamberlain's, the joint firm keeping only the title of 'Chamberlain and Co.' W. H. Kerr joined the company in 1850, and in 1852, on the retirement of Chamberlain, R. W. Binns entered into a partnership with Kerr and the firm was conducted in the name of 'Kerr and Binns'.

Kerr retired in 1862 and the company then became known as the Worcester Royal Porcelain Works and this is the name which appears in the Crowned W mark of the time. The Grainger firm continued as a separate organization until 1889 when it was finally absorbed by the principal company.

Worcester during the Victorian era was distinguished in many ways, notably for the production of enamelled porcelain in the style of Limoges, and in the hands of Thomas Bott some exquisitely painted vases, dishes and ewers were made. These early acquired collector status, and even in the 1870's a pair of Bott's enamelled vases was already valued at 1,500 guineas.

Under the artistic directorship of Binns Worcester also achieved eminence in several other fields, particularly in 'ivory porcelain', an ivory tinted and softly glazed body, and in 'jewelled porcelain' which, while derived from the 'jewelled' style of Sèvres, was manufactured by a different process. At Sèvres the 'jewels' were of enamel and simply applied to the surface of the vase or plate by a fixative. The Worcester 'jewels' were incorporated into the porcelain itself, being blobs of colour fired with the actual body of the piece. This 'jewelled china' was very much admired at the Paris Exhibition of 1867.

Under the Chamberlain régime Japanese influence had already been apparent in the various 'Japan' patterns, in the manner of Crown Derby, produced at Worcester from about 1800 to roughly 1840. The colouring was generally less satisfactory than that of Derby, neither the blue nor the gold being nearly as attractive, while the pieces as a whole tended to be too close in design to their Japanese originals, not imaginative versions of them, as the Derby patterns often were. Sometimes, too, a Japanese border would be combined with an English armorial central design, and this, however meticulously painted, produced an inartistic combination hardly worthy of so famous a firm. Worcester under Binns continued to produce many Japanese designs, including vases, trays, *jardinières* and many other articles 'in the Japanese taste'. A particularly interesting set of vases showed the various processes of the craft of pottery, the groups being modelled in relief by Hadley, and painted and gilded by Callowhill.

Above: 1. Pair of Minton pedestal vases painted by Thomas Allen. *Below:* 2. Pair of Minton vases with stands; one with Leda and the Swan painted by Henk after Boucher, the other by Boullemier: mid-Victorian.

Above: 3. Royal Crown Derby teaware with 'Mikado' pattern; blue and white with gold rims: late Victorian. *Below:* 4. Part of a Copeland and Garrett tea and coffee service: 1833–35.

5. Chamberlain's Worcester plate in 'Imari' style, decorated in deep blue, tomato-colour and gold: c.1840.

6. Booth's plate; copy of Dr Wall's Worcester 'Scale Blue and Birds' with raised gold decoration: Edwardian.

7. Mason's two-handled ironstone vase in oriental style: c. 1850.

8. Worcester vase in Japanese style, simulating bronze-mounted carved ivory.

9. Worcester vase; pâte-sur-pâte on pink ground: 1880.

10. Mason's ironstone vase in oriental style, with dragon handles and finial: c. 1850.

11. Tall pâte-sur-pâte Minton vase in deep turquoise by Solon entitled 'The Toy Seller'; pattern number NP 1164: 1899.

Left: 12. Worcester cake plate with gadrooned edge, in royal blue and raised gold; reserves and centre painted with flowers: 1902. *Right:* 13. Worcester saucer painted with flowers and ribbons with crowned W mark: 1862–70.

Left: 14. Chamberlain's Worcester plate decorated in tomato-colour and gold: c. 1835–40. *Right:* 15. Rockingham plate; deep blue ground with gilt edges and central floral spray: c. 1840.

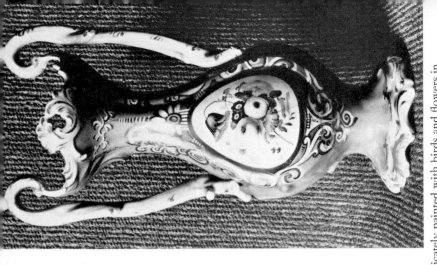

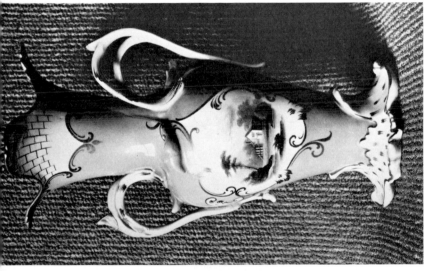

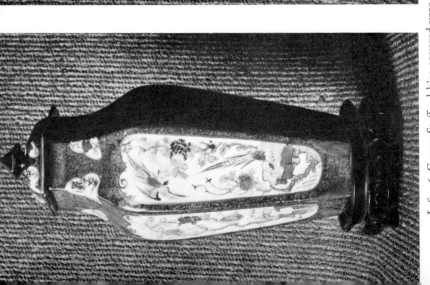

Left: 16. Crown Staffordshire covered vase in Chinese style; powder blue ground with panels delicately painted with birds and flowers in shades of rose and green: Edwardian. *Centre:* 17. Vase, possibly Coalport; apple-green ground with light gilding and landscape panel in shades of brown and green: registration mark for 1842. *Right:* 18. Vase, possibly Rockingham; apple-green ground with delicate gilding and gracefully painted flowers: c. 1840.

Left: 19. Davenport plate showing influence of Derby 'Imari' designs; deep blue with brilliant gilding and tomato-coloured motifs: late Victorian. *Right:* 20. Coalport plate in 'Rose Pompadour', with raised gold and reserves and central medallion of finely painted flowers: c. 1850

21. Worcester vase modelled by J. Hadley: one of a pair embodying groups of pottery craftsmen after Picolpasso: 1878.

22. Worcester vase modelled by J. Hadley in 'Ivory Porcelain', decorated in 'Raphaelesque' style by S. T. Callowhill: 1877.

Above: 23. Worcester flower tube comport and two pierced dessert plates from service made for Queen Victoria in 1861. The painted decoration by Thomas Bott is in the style of Limoges enamel on a turquoise blue ground and the embossments are richly gilded. *Left:* 24. Worcester vase modelled by J. Hadley and decorated in gold by S. Ranford: 1880.

Left: 25. Copeland vase decorated by C. F. Hürten, celebrated as one of the best flower painters of his time: 1889. *Below:* 26. Worcester 'Parian' salt from the 'Shakespeare' service (1853) and Worcester 'Parian' inkwell (c. 1855), both modelled by W. B. Kirk.

27. Minton 'Parian' figure, *Miranda*, by John Bell: shape number 245, impressed year mark for 1866.

28. Copeland 'Parian' bust of Queen Victoria made during her Golden Jubilee year: 1887.

Above: 29. Minton plaque painted by Daniel Lucas (possibly Copeland): mid-Victorian. *Below:* 30. Worcester card tray 13¼ inches by 8⅞ inches, with modelled applied shells surrounding a painted scene of the new 'Houses of Parliament': c. 1845.

Above: 31. Two Copeland plates with views of Richmond Bridge and Maidstone, Kent: c. 1830. *Below:* 32. Copeland plate painted with a view of the Castle of Comares with a border decorated with gold: 1851.

The artistic achievements of Japan were, however, not generally known in Europe until the 1860's when the London Exhibition of 1862 and the Paris Exhibition of 1867 created a sudden wave of enthusiastic interest in them. Whistler's famous 'Porcelain Princess' is an early example of the influence of Japanese subjects on Western painters, and it was not long before Japanese designs for porcelain became extremely popular in England. Worcester was one of the first of the great firms to exploit this enthusiasm and, using a warm ivory tinted body, they produced a fine series of pieces which simulated Japanese ivories and bronzes with remarkably faithful, perhaps too faithful skill. For the general effect is of an exact reproduction of ivory and bronze rather than of an object constructed of porcelain.

'Persian' and 'Indian' style vases were also made in large quantities, many of them of exquisite beauty and certainly worth careful attention from the collector if they can be encountered.

Victorian Worcester also produced figures, busts and groups in Parian ware and in ivory-tinted porcelain, which continued to be much praised at the various international exhibitions of the latter half of the century. At Chicago in 1893, for instance, the Worcester exhibits of this kind were particularly praised for 'the sharpness of the modelling' and 'the artistic character of the designs'.

One of the most brilliant virtuoso accomplishments of Worcester during the nineteenth century was the remarkable 'reticulated' work of George Owen, whose hand-pierced vases are triumphs of technical skill. Bands of reticulations of diapers in a honeycomb formation produced the effect of a vase made entirely of lace, with walls of an astonishing thinness.

At the extreme end of the Victorian period came a short-lived development from the Royal Porcelain Works which was to be in a few years again absorbed by it. This was the venture of James Hadley, who had for some time been chief modeller with the great firm and in 1896 launched into his own business in Worcester, the pieces produced by him being known as 'Hadley Ware'. This separate venture lasted only until 1905, when the Royal Porcelain Company took control of it, but it is of interest to collectors since

D

some very individual work was done by it and specimens are well worth acquiring. In the earlier work raised decoration in coloured clays was used, sometimes with paintings either in monochrome or colours, and later on the pieces were ornamented in enamels and gold. Tea-, dinner- and breakfast-services were made in a very wide variety of patterns, but the vases, especially those with raised flowers, are the most interesting. They have a *fin-de-siècle* elegance and grace of modelling which, to those who like suggestive overtones in their collecting, is richly redolent of the drawing-rooms of the Beardsley and Wilde era, and of the opening years of the Edwardian age.

The Hadley pieces produced by the separate firm are quite clearly marked with their own name, but 'Hadley Ware' after 1905 has the usual contemporary Royal Worcester mark.

While he was still at the Royal factory Hadley had been responsible for some remarkably fine pieces, including some intricate 'Japanese' style vases and the celebrated 'Potter' vase showing two potters at work, marvellously modelled in relief, and a splendid 'nef' in Italian style. The 'potter' vases (there were a pair) were very highly praised when shown in Paris at the 1878 Exhibition; replicas of them are now in the Royal Porcelain Works Museum.

R. L. Hobson, in his monumental work 'Worcester Porcelain' (1910) quotes the comments of the 'Guide through the Worcester Royal Porcelain Works' on the general characteristics of Hadley's technique and style. It tells how he got his effects 'by means of an extensive use of coloured clays in the raised ornamentation of the vase, etc., combined with either a monochrome or a conventional treatment of the subject paintings. Latterly, without losing the distinctive qualities of the ware, the severity of this early style had gradually given way to a less conventional one, and for much of the coloured clay work there are now substituted various decorative schemes in enamel colours and gold, with fully naturalistic treatment, both as regards colour and composition for the subject paintings, thus supplying the artist with a much wider field of work than obtained during the earlier periods of the ware'.

The Grainger Works at Worcester was never a really serious

rival to the principal company, but it achieved some distinguished work and made a notable contribution to ceramic history by the invention of 'semi-porcelain', which was first on view to the general public at the Crystal Palace in 1851, and was awarded a medal at the Exhibition of 1862. This was a highly vitrified form of china, much more heat-resistant than normal porcelain, and so better suited for dinner-services and any other objects liable to be subjected to heat. It had also a natural toughness which made breakage far less likely, and a considerable trade was done by the firm in the manufacture of vessels for chemical purposes in this material, such pieces being marked 'Chemical Porcelain. Grainger and Co. Manufactory, Worcester'.

Grainger's also developed a technically very accomplished 'perforated Parian ware' in which a lace-like effect was produced by elaborate perforations of the surface in geometrical and other designs. Pieces incorporating Grainger's 'ceramic lace drapery' also became famous and are now worth the collector's notice. Another speciality of Grainger's was a material known as opalite which formed a high-quality vitrifiable body suitable for embossed tiles for domestic decoration.

Grainger's produced a quantity of costly-looking but reasonably priced ware, as in the coffee-service of 1851, described as 'a light and elegant service for the boudoir'. This had an open honeycomb pattern set in a rich blue ground, the handles and borders of the tray decorated with wheat-ears, together with their stalks and leaves.

In addition to the Grainger and Hadley works at Worcester there was a third firm, though it practised only on a small scale and closed after a few years. This was Locke and Company, which was in operation for some ten years from 1895 when a lawsuit with the Royal Porcelain Works concerning the use of the word 'Worcester' ended unfavourably for the Lockes.

Edward Locke was the founder of this works, having himself worked at the main factory in Worcester for a time, and his pieces were very much in the style of the main factory. His establishment was at Shrub Hill, and his products bear the inscription

'Locke and Co., Worcester, England' with the addition of the words 'Shrub Hill Works' after 1900.

The collector will be certain sooner or later to encounter imitations of Worcester's famous 'scale blue and exotic birds' designs which had reached such perfection in the Dr Wall period. Thousands of these were produced during the Victorian period, as much abroad as in England, and they were of very varied quality. Some were rank forgeries, complete with forged marks; others, however, were of first-class quality and very high technical accomplishment. Among the latter must be accounted the charming work produced by Booth's which was really a very pleasant and quite honest attempt to revive the Worcester style without any attempt to simulate their factory marks.

Specimens of these pieces crop up at sales from time to time, and single plates, presenting a good reproduction of the celebrated scale-blue and birds pattern, with well-executed bird and floral painting and with meticulous raised gold decoration, can often be bought for two or three pounds each, the smaller ones for even less. The gilding (at least on the examples I have) is a little brassy, and the plumage of the 'exotic birds' less mellow and harmonious than on their famous Worcester prototypes, but they still make delightful wall-plates.

A whole range of pieces was produced in this pattern, including some graceful vases, pierced dishes, bowls, candlesticks, small covered boxes and teapots as well as the more frequently encountered plates and cups and saucers. Many of them date from the Edwardian era and they are usually quite plainly marked 'Booth's', though some have no mark at all.

DERBY

At the beginning of the Victorian era the classic period of Derby porcelain was already drawing to a disastrous close. Robert Bloor, the last of a famous line of Derby proprietors, became mentally deranged about 1828, and the quality of the work produced under his management rapidly deteriorated. Another cause of the deterioration was the quantity of imperfect pieces which Bloor had inherited from his predecessors and which were stored away at the works. Bloor was tempted to touch these up and sell them by auction, and this proved so profitable that the temptation to go on producing goods mainly for auction purposes without bestowing too much care on their finish was so great that it was allowed to continue, to the damage of the factory's reputation.

Bloor, however, lingered on until 1845, but in 1848 the works finally closed down. A dispersal of the workmen and artists inevitably followed, some going to Staffordshire, others to Worcester, but a small nucleus of them remained in Derby where, in fresh premises in King Street, and under the title of 'Locker and Co., late Bloor', they continued to produce 'Derby china'.

A number of changes of management followed Locker's death in 1859, including 'Stevenson and Co.', 'Stevenson, Sharp and Co.', and the Stevenson and Hancock management which is commemorated in the frequently seen mark on Victorian pieces, an S and H flanking dotted crossed swords over a D, the whole surmounted by a crown.

In 1876 an event of outstanding importance occurred, the founding of the present Royal Crown Derby Porcelain Company, though it did not assume the title 'Royal' until 1890 when Queen Victoria granted a warrant of appointment to the firm as 'Manufacturers of Porcelain to the Crown'. This new scheme for the large-scale revival of porcelain making at Derby originated with the former manager of the Worcester Royal Porcelain Works, Edward Phillips, who, together with William Litherland and John McInnes, formed a limited liability company with a capital of £67,850. In 1875 a completely new works was erected on the Osmaston Road, and, after a temporary stay in Chetwynd Street pending the completion of this factory, the company opened operations in their fresh home in 1877.

From the first the products of the new firm attracted great and widespread admiration, and the highest in the land, including Queen Victoria herself, the late Queen Mary (then known as Princess May) and other distinguished patrons became devoted admirers of its work. Gladstone was particularly enthusiastic about it when, in 1883, he was given a handsome dessert service 'designed and manufactured by the Derby Crown Porcelain Co. Limited, for presentation to the Right Honble W. E. Gladstone, M.P., by the Liberal Working Men of Derby'.

This sumptuous service, which incorporated Gladstone's initials in reserved panels alternating with delicate floral motifs, even inspired the great statesman to proclaim, in his speech of thanks to the delegation, his belief that at that moment England stood at the very head of the porcelain producing countries of the world. There was certainly much justification for this claim, as anyone must admit who cares to compare our own late Victorian porcelain with that produced by France or Germany or Italy, or indeed any other country during the same years.

The splendid gift to Gladstone was followed, a few years later, by an equally magnificent present to the Queen on the occasion of her Golden Jubilee in 1887. This consisted of two superb vases and a circular plaque, the vases of mazarine blue, richly gilded and painted, and the plaque in the form of a portrait of the Queen, decorated with quarterings of the Royal Arms, together with the shields of the twenty-four colonies in their correct heraldic colours.

Yet another magnificent gift was the wedding present to the late Queen Mary when, as Princess May, she married in 1893 the Duke of York, afterwards King George V. This was a set of plates, in turquoise and gold, with flowers and medallions and the floral monogram of G.M. surmounted by a raised gold crown and the heraldic arms of the House of York.

From this time onwards the revived Derby works, fortified with its new title of 'Royal' (the warrant being immediately renewed by Edward VII in 1901), has continued to the present day to produce fine work, including the well-known 'Crown Derby Japan pattern' which, with its rich gilding and deep blue and tomato-coloured motifs, is still as popular as ever it was. Apparently this pattern is very much prized by wealthy gipsies and a number of the most expensive pieces still ultimately find their way into caravan homes. The pattern is not a late Victorian development for 'Crown Derby Japan' designs were produced in great variety during the first half of the nineteenth century; they remained extremely popular right up to the closing of the original works in 1848. Their inspiration was apparently the Japanese 'brocade' designs known as Imari, though this was in fact only the port of Japan from which they were shipped to Europe. Dutch traders of the seventeenth century seem to have provided the original impetus for the manufacture of these designs; they are said to have been the first to persuade the Japanese potters to make use of their magnificent brocades for ceramic decoration.

Derby was foremost in the field in adapting these designs to its own use, and though 'Derby Japan' patterns have always tended to be more fussy in detail than the true Imaris there is no doubt that they have considerable beauty and have richly deserved their popularity. The design has, however, been unfortunately vulgarized by the innumerable cheap copies which have been made, usually characterized by uncertainty of touch (the Derby pieces are always meticulously done) and crudity of colour. In the genuine examples the blue is deep and evenly laid, with a rich tomato-orange, delicate touches of green, and brilliant gilding. The patterns have always been expensive to produce, but their ready sale stimulated many other factories to experiment with similar designs. Some splendid pieces in this style were, for example, turned out by Davenport in the later nineteenth century; I recently picked up one of their plates from a market stall which clearly shows the 'Derby Japan' influence. Both the gilding and the ground colours, a rich *bleu-du-roi* and a tomato-orange (somewhat paler than the Derby colour, but very well laid), are excellent, and it might even be said that the design is nearer in spirit to the original Imari 'brocades' than those of Derby. There is a central gold floral motif from which radiate ten segmental panels, five in tomato-orange and five in *bleu-du-roi*, each richly gilded and yet not too much smothered in gold. The brilliance of the gilding has not been in the least impaired by time, the glaze has a lustrous softness and the potting is impeccable.

When the new Derby company was formed in 1876 it was determined to revive and repopularize the most successful designs of the earlier firm, and certainly none of its patterns has achieved more lasting success than the 'Crown Derby Japan'. In fact this pattern has come to be associated in many people's minds so closely with Derby that they tend to think of it as the only style which the later works produced. But of course many other beautiful styles were revived, and fresh ones developed, by the new company from 1876 onwards. The styles of Sèvres, Chelsea, and Derby's own older work, were often beautifully rendered in modern adaptations, the work of the painter Désiré Leroy being especially notable in the handsome Sèvres-style vases produced in the last decade of Victoria's reign.

Leroy had been trained at Sèvres, and one of his first important commissions after joining the Derby works in 1890 was the fine set of royal wedding plates referred to above. His subsequent superb Sèvres-style vases, magnificently painted with birds and flowers, on grounds of mazarine blue, celadon and ivory, enriched with raised and chased gold, recall the glories of Sèvres itself in its greatest days. Anyone fortunate enough to acquire any of the authenticated works of Leroy will have made an acquisition which must appreciate in value as time goes on.

Leroy, in addition to his Sèvres-style painting, also produced some interesting works in white enamel on a gorund of cobalt, the effect being similar to that of *pâte-sur-pâte*.

ROCKINGHAM

The Rockingham works closed in 1842 so that their porcelain only enters into the very beginning of the Victorian era. But many of its characteristics clearly foreshadowed later Victorian styles, notably the over-elaborate decoration of the vases and their frequent ungainliness of shape.

Porcelain was not introduced into the Rockingham programme until 1820, and the manufacture of it only got into its stride about 1825 so that the entire period of its making is less than a quarter of a century, and it had very little time in which to develop its own character and eliminate its own faults. Many people find its elaboration overpowering, but whatever criticism may be passed on its decorative qualities none can well be made of the superb paste itself, a magnificent bone-porcelain of faultless texture and exquisite glaze. No expense was spared to make Rockingham porcelain worthy to compete with the great achievements of the past, and in the end the Brameld family, in spite of the patronage of their landlord, Earl Fitzwilliam, found themselves in great financial straits owing to their uneconomic methods. The commercial crisis of 1825 certainly contributed to their downfall, but the lavish expenditure on the work at Rockingham seems to have been the real cause of the disaster of 1842 when production ceased and the entire stock was sold. Even the famous dessert service made for the King himself in 1830 had been produced at a considerable loss, though the price (a high one considering the contemporary value of money) was five thousand pounds for the 144 plates and 56 other pieces.

Other expensive services were made for the Duchess of Cumberland in 1830 and for the Duke of Sussex in 1833, also for the King of Hanover and the King of the Belgians. Neither these, however, nor many other lavish orders from 'the quality' could stem the tide of financial embarrassment; in fact, the production of some of these services seems to have been purely prestige work owing to the costs involved. The plates in the royal dessert service, for instance, had both dead and burnished gold with gorgeously painted centres; the comports and ice pails were adorned with ears of wheat and holly berries; magnificent views of various mansions, groups of flowers and medallions of the Royal Arms, surrounded by the most splendid raised gilding, decorated the sumptuous plates, each one of which, even in the money of the time, was most costly to produce.

The whole history of Rockingham's 'porcelain period', indeed, reads like a miniature history of Sèvres in the pre-Revolution years in France, with a mounting tide of reckless magnificence which could never hope to pay its way.

An outstanding example of the firm's lavishness was the great vase which Earl Fitzwilliam possessed at Wentworth House and to which the overworked epithet 'fabulous' could for once be correctly applied. This remarkable object, which was 3 feet 9 inches tall, had a tripod-shaped base, blue with floral decoration and heavily gilded, and the vase itself, on white and gold lion's paws, was a sumptuous composition with elaborate scenes from 'Don Quixote', the cover being splendidly painted with flowers, trophies, oak leaves, and golden acorns. Even the underside was painted with landscapes, and the finial, grotesque but gorgeous, was a superbly gilded rhinoceros.

Wentworth House also contained many other examples of Rockingham pieces and seems to have been a kind of 'Works Museum' in some ways, for there were such things as a breakfast-service painted with flowers, a fine tray painted with a view of Arundel Castle, 'monkey' beakers, porcelain scent bottles, a white and gold dessert-service in the 'seaweed' pattern, and many specimen plates of varying degrees of glittering splendour.

Other private collections housed some of the grandiose 'dragon' vases, dragon-handled and dragon-covered, and the lovely green and gold swan-handled vases, finely painted with Italian views of Bellagio, Verona, and Isola Bella, and the 'English country mansion' pieces with views of Newstead, Chatsworth, etc.

And among the more interesting curiosities of nineteenth-century ceramic art were the Rockingham china bed-posts, which were first made in 1838. The colouring of these seems to have been largely Rose Pompadour with yellow flowers, though some had a white ground with multi-coloured floral motifs. Not many of these can have survived since few were made, but if the collector encounters any they would be well worth buying.

The Rockingham works was actually sited at Swinton in Yorkshire, and a number of the older books on porcelain list it as 'Swinton'. It owes the title of 'Rockingham' to the Marquis of Rockingham, some of whose land at Swinton was used as far back as 1745 for the extraction of clays suitable for pottery, firebricks and tiles. Up to 1826 the proprietors themselves called their works 'Swinton'. But when Brameld, the senior partner in the firm, decided on the addition of porcelain to the Swinton programme the name became definitely 'Rockingham' and from the first every effort was made to see that the new Rockingham paste should be as perfect as experiment could make it. In the management of the firm were some other members of the Brameld family as well as the senior partner, Thomas. G. F. Brameld, for instance, was responsible for the Russian export branch of the company and lived for a time at St Petersburg, while J. W. Brameld, who combined travelling duties with the painting of porcelain, must have been one of the hardest worked of all.

The Bramelds engaged some of the best modellers and painters of the day as soon as the porcelain department opened, among whom was John Presswell, and the original works at Swinton were considerably enlarged and improved.

Owing to the shortness of the firm's porcelain period (it was only about seventeen years in full production) specimens are naturally not very numerous in comparison with other longer-lived works. This alone will always tend to give Rockingham pieces a certain scarcity value and any collector who is able to build up a representative assemblage of them may consider himself extremely fortunate.

Chapter Three

Other Firms: I

BERNARD MOORE

OUTSTANDING among individual porcelain artists of the nineteenth century was Bernard Moore, chiefly famous for his wonderful work in reproducing the Chinese *flambé* glazes with consummate artistic skill. Using a wide range of colours, Moore produced an equally wide range of designs, including various kinds of vases and *jardinières*, all superbly clad in *flambé* glazes of differing shades of red, sometimes light, sometimes ruby, and in black, brown, *sang-de-bœuf*, palest grey, and gold.

The celebrated *sang-de-bœuf* glaze of the Chinese potters had been admired in England, and indeed in all Europe, for many years. Many attempts had been made to copy it, but it was Bernard Moore who succeeded best in overcoming the great technical difficulties of reproducing it artistically. The firing necessary for the production of *sang-de-bœuf* red has to be conducted in an air from which oxygen has been excluded, and each piece had to be virtually a separate work of art since mass production was quite impossible.

A most beautiful 'splashed' or mottled effect is produced by the *flambé* glazes, which were obtained by the use of oxide of copper and other metals. Exquisite transmutations of colouring were achieved in many of the pieces; some of the smaller vases in rouge *flambé* (veined red), decorated with turquoise and gold-outlined dragon and peacock designs, must be reckoned among the loveliest examples of nineteenth-century ceramic art.

Bernard Moore was not an isolated artist working from a private studio. He was one of two brothers, trading as 'Moore Bros', who in 1870 succeeded their father as joint owners of the St Mary's

Works at Longton, Stoke-on-Trent, which had been founded as far back as 1830. The two brothers soon established a high reputation for the quality of their glazes, particularly their 'Persian turquoise glaze'. They also produced some fine *cloisonné* enamels, often richly gilded, and some Japanese-style designs.

Many of Moore Bros pieces were marked with the name of T. Goode and Co., the London dealers. A collection of their work would be well worth making, though the much admired and sought-after *flambé* pieces later produced by Bernard himself are unlikely to come the collector's way except at a very high price.

GOSS

The collector of Victorian porcelain should not overlook the work of Goss, in spite of the firm's vast outpouring of those trivial armorial pieces for ever associated with its name and sold as souvenirs in so many English towns. Goss during the Victorian age (the firm was founded in 1858) also manufactured many beautiful vases and Parian busts, as well as 'porcelain jewellery' such as brooches, hair-pins, scent-diffusers, and ear-rings, and the ivory porcelain paste used for much of their work was of considerable delicacy and charm. In this connection Goss took out a patent 'for improvements in manufacturing articles of jewellery, dress ornaments, dress fastenings, smoke shades for lamps and gas burners, and the handles of cups and other vessels of ceramic materials'.

W. Gallimore, an artist from the Irish factory of Belleek, modelled some of the best of the Parian busts, including one of Llewellyn Jewitt, the author of the monumental 'Ceramic Art in Great Britain', published in 1878; this forms the frontispiece to his book. Another fine work by Gallimore was a bust of S. C. Hall, the editor of the *Art Journal*.

Of Gallimore Jewitt quaintly says 'He at one time was engaged as a modeller at the Belleek Works in Ireland, and while there, by the bursting of a gun, lost his right arm. His modelling has, therefore, ever since then been entirely done by his left hand, and, strange as it may seem, is far better than when he had both.'

Goss also produced a very wide variety of scent-vases, pastille-burners, pomade boxes and perfume-containers, these last being specially made for the principal London and Paris perfumiers.

Goss's 'jewelled porcelain' is of considerable interest since it was technically an improvement on the earlier method as developed at Sèvres. The imitation rubies and emeralds of Sèvres were applied after the porcelain had been fired, being merely fixed on with a flux and then subjected to a further firing. Often the 'jewels' did not fix on satisfactorily, and would come off in time, but Goss perfected a new method whereby special cavities for the reception of the jewels were first made in the porcelain itself before firing, and this then made for perfect security.

BELLEEK

The porcelain produced at Belleek has attracted considerable attention of recent years and the value of its finer pieces is likely to rise steadily. Belleek was the only porcelain works of any consequence in Ireland during the nineteenth century, and it owed its inception to a tour of the country made by Kerr, of the Worcester Royal Porcelain Works, and his architect, R. W. Armstrong, with a view to finding supplies of Irish clay which could be utilized at Worcester in the manufacture of their own porcelain.

Trials of the felspar found in the Belleek district were made at Worcester, and gave such fine results that Armstrong decided, with the help of a Dublin enthusiast, David McBirney, to found a works at Belleek itself. In 1857 (some writers believe the date to be 1863) the factory was opened and rapidly rose to prosperity. One of its earliest noble patrons was Queen Victoria herself, and she purchased from Belleek a tea-service for presentation to the Empress of Germany which incorporated in its design the 'echinus', or sea-urchin which is found on the seacoast of Donegal.

This was a foretaste of much to come, since sea shells, branches of coral, and other forms of marine decoration were to enter prominently into Belleek designs. The *Art Journal* drew attention to the originality of many of these, and made some interesting comparisons in the course of its notice:

'The reproduction of natural forms by Ceramic Art is not by any means a novelty. We are familiar with the fish, the reptiles, and the crustacea of Bernard Palissy, with the relieved and coloured foliage of Luca and of Andrea della Robbia. In England we have seen the shells reproduced by the artists of the Plymouth china, and the delicate leaves and flowers of the old Derby ware. The designer of much of the Belleek ware has the merit, so far as we are aware, of being the first artist who has had recourse to the large sub-kingdom of the *radiata* for his types. The animals that constitute this vast natural group are, for the most part, characterized by a star-shaped or wheel-shaped symmetry; and present a nearer approach to the verticillate structure of plants, than to the bilateral balance of free locomotive animals.'

With typical Victorian thoroughness the writer goes on to describe learnedly the 'zoophytic' creatures, the echinus, and the *frutti di mare*, or sea-eggs, and to praise the Belleek artists for bringing them into the service of ceramic art. Mermaids, nereids, dolphins, and sea-horses were also used as decorative motifs, as in the characteristically Victorian 'boudoir flower shells' which were one of the firm's most admired products. 'Marine decoration' was used too in the handsome service made for the Prince of Wales, a most elaborate piece being the Ice Pail, in which three Parian mermaids form the support to the pail which is decorated with tritons and dolphins in relief. A border of coral runs round the rim, with sea-horses and another Triton forming the cover. The comports also incorporated cardium shells, mermaids, trumpet-shells, and tritons blowing on conches.

In addition to these marine motifs, which were widely used by Belleek in many of their other services and individual pieces, the firm produced an extensive range of dinner-, breakfast-, tea-, and dessert-services of more conventional patterns; also many figures

and animals and 'cabinet' cups and saucers of an astonishing lightness of texture.

A very notable feature of Belleek porcelain was the fine iridesc-
ent glaze which, united to the ivory-cream colour of the paste,
produced effects of great delicacy and charm. The *Art Journal*
enthusiastically praised the lustrous mother-of-pearl quality of
the Belleek glaze, comparing it with the ruby lustre of the Gubbio
majolica, and it certainly had a unique beauty which will continue
to make its better examples highly prized.

The earlier work of the firm was undoubtedly the best. Armstrong himself died in 1884, and though the factory continued in
production after his death the quality of the goods deteriorated.
The secret of the famous glaze passed into the possession of
Armstrong's sons, and on the sale of the works to another company it remained in their hands, but it is not known with any cer-
tainty what final use was made of it.

CAULDON PLACE

The celebrated Ridgway works at Cauldon Place date from 1802
and they were continued by members of the Ridgway family until
1855, when the business was acquired by the firm known as
'T. C. Brown-Westhead, Moore and Co.' Moore had been one of
the principal assistants to the younger Ridgway, and on his death
in 1866 he was followed in the firm by his brother and son.

Both porcelain and earthenware were produced at Cauldon
Place in very great quantities, and the firm's list ranged from the
most utilitarian sanitary ware (including drinking fountains) to
splendid porcelain dessert services, such as those made for the
Prince of Wales, decorated with hunting scenes, for the Imperial
Russian family, for the Emperor of Morocco, and for the Duchess
of Edinburgh to her own designs.

The Ridgway period at Cauldon Place was notable for a
number of technical experiments, including improvements in the
construction of moulds, and, in 1852, the application of electro-
metallurgy in the decorative processes of both porcelain and

earthenware. Awards were made to the firm at the Crystal Palace and at Paris in 1855, and to their successors at the London Exhibition of 1862, at Lyons in 1872, Vienna in 1873, and at the Philadelphia Exhibition of 1876 where they had a very extensive show. In 1884 they rivalled Copelands at Paris, both firms gaining the Grand Prix.

The 1851 award set a seal on the already quite considerable success of the firm, and the *Art Journal* of that year devoted a long notice to their work. Their utilitarian ware was highly praised since 'although the usefulness of these articles has been the primary consideration, their elegance has also been properly cared for, and they are really graceful additions to the dressing-room, free of the trouble attendant on the use of the ordinary ewer and basin'. The simplicity of much of the decoration on their pieces was also singled out for special praise; no doubt it was a refreshing novelty amidst the jungle of riotous ornamentation which characterized so much of the work at the Crystal Palace.

The work of Ridgways, and equally of Brown-Westhead, Moore and Co., was notable for its durability and toughness of texture, while the colours were very evenly laid, their Rose Pompadour and maroon being of high quality and their jewelling and gilding usually meticulous. Jewitt notes several interesting designs of the Brown-Westhead, Moore period, such as a sandwich box of white china, composed of wicker-work in porcelain, with a fernleaf across the lid supporting a butterfly which forms the handle. Both this and an 'elegant basket', with the handle formed as a double knotted cord, are praised for their 'purity and simplicity'.

A 'Rose du Barry' cup and saucer, again with cord and knot decoration, and embossed with gold, is also praised as 'peculiarly elegant', while the patent self-acting cover for hot-water jugs which Jewitt describes shows that the firm was still interested in producing novel utilitarian pieces as well as the more ornamental ware.

It would be interesting to build up a collection of the many different articles produced by Ridgways and Brown-Westhead,

Moore and Co. Their range was so great that any representative assembly of their goods would cover many facets of Victorian domestic life. It would, besides, throw valuable sidelights on the commercial life of the times, for they produced 'improved' druggists' and perfumiers' articles as well as the mysterious 'Toilettes Victoria' which were 'used by the Imperial family and elsewhere in Paris', so Jewitt tantalizingly records.

MADELEY

The china produced by the little Madeley manufactory only enters the Victorian period at the close of its life, for the originator and owner, T. M. Randall, left Madeley in 1840 and no more ware was made there. But the works are of great interest to the student of Victorian porcelain since they were a centre for the production of some marvellously delicate work in the manner of Sèvres; their success no doubt stimulated many of the other factories, such as Coalport and Mintons, to develop their own imitations of Sèvres shortly after the Madeley enterprises closed down.

Randall had, in fact, served his apprenticeship at Coalport, going on to Derby from there and subsequently to London where, with a partner from Pinxton, he set up a small business as a decorator of porcelain. This business included the painting of genuine Sèvres pieces which had been bought up by dealers such as Baldock and Garman, either undecorated or very slightly painted, at the great sale at Sèvres in 1813. Wherever possible white china was used, but a number of pieces with single lines and small sprigs of flowers were also bought, the designs being removed by hydrofluoric acid and fresh paintings applied.

Randall left London in 1826 and soon afterwards established his small works at Madeley where, until 1840, he produced some of the most charming porcelain of the entire nineteenth century. The paste itself was of a beautiful glassy texture with a splendid glaze, rich and mellow, though Randall had suffered much inconvenience and many losses in its manufacture owing to his lack of technical experience.

But he ultimately produced an extremely fine paste, closely resembling that of Sèvres. This served as an excellent base for his beautiful turquoise colouring, resembling the famous Persian turquoise, which, together with gorgeous gold scrolling and panels painted with figures, birds and flowers, soon established the fame of Madeley with the London dealers.

The production of the Madeley pieces was, however, very expensive, and in 1840 Randall decided to close the works, removing to Shelton where he continued decorating, still in the manner of Sèvres, until 1856. His reputation was such that he even received an offer from Mintons to manufacture and decorate his own porcelain at their works in Stoke-on-Trent, but he declined. He was a strict Quaker and, though many of his pieces could pass for genuine Sèvres, he always refused to imitate the Sèvres mark and since he used no mark of his own the identification of his work is extremely difficult. Authenticated Madeley specimens are, however, most certainly worth the collector's attention if he can find any, and an assemblage of Randall's turquoise and gold pieces would make a most beautiful and increasingly valuable collection.

DAVENPORT

The history of the Davenport firm goes back to 1773 when it was founded at Longport by John Brindley, passing twenty years later into the Davenport family. The first Davenport, John, was a man of considerable public spirit, a Major of the Volunteers at the time of the threatened Napoleonic invasion and ultimately M.P. for the new Parliamentary Constituency of Stoke-on-Trent.

Other members of the family afterwards owned the works which in 1873 celebrated its centenary, though it finally ceased production in the 1880's.

Early successes for Davenports included a commission from William the Fourth to produce his Coronation Banquet service, and the lustre bestowed on the works by this considerably stimulated their foreign trade. Depots were subsequently opened at

Lübeck and Hamburg, and an important commerce established with dealers in Brazil. As a result of this commission Davenports for a time used the crown over their name as part of their mark.

The Brindley works had confined itself to earthenware and glass-making, and during the earlier years of the Davenport régime the products were mostly simple earthenware also, but there was also some blue-printed ware similar to that made by Adams and the Herculaneum Works at Liverpool. Later on porcelain was added and this, during the Victorian period, rose to a high degree of excellence.

The paste used was a mixture of clay and china stone with bone ash, the glaze containing boracic acid, alkalis and lead oxide.

Davenport gilding was rich and lustrous, lavishly applied to handles, rims and feet, and in their versions of the 'Japan' patterns they closely rivalled the prototypes which Derby had made so famous. Their blues and reds, combined with their magnificent gold, make a splendid show, especially in their plates and cups, the colours being excellently and very evenly laid. The Davenport deep blue was particularly successful, and only slightly less so were their celadon and a very beautiful apple-green. Rich gilding was also employed in the Davenport adaptations of the Willow Pattern, and, though this may well seem to some tastes an almost literal gilding of the lily, to those who like their Victorian porcelain with a true flavour of Victorian lavishness services in this style will have a strong appeal.

In the general reaction against Victoriana, from which we have now almost completely recovered, much criticism was levelled against porcelain of the Davenport school, and even at the present date the firm's reputation has not fully survived the onslaught. Their richness of decoration has seemed to some to represent the quintessence of Victorian over-elaboration, while the generally expensive appearance of so many of their dessert-, tea- and coffee-services has often been dismissed as tasteless and ill-conceived. Such opinions are, however, much less heard now than formerly. It would surely be difficult to maintain, at this time of day, that the best of the Davenport pieces, especially their finer plates and comports with scroll borders in gold and meticulously painted with fruit, were anything but a credit to the art of English porcelain.

But it is still possible to obtain good specimens fairly cheaply, and anyone looking for a particular works on which to specialize in his collecting might do well to consider making an assemblage of Davenport.

OLD HALL (MEIGH'S)

The Old Hall factory at Hanley dates back to 1770 when it was founded by Job Meigh, but its very industrious Victorian activities are what concern us here, and these are of special interest in the years around 1851, when more than 700 people were in full employment there. Both the Crystal Palace and the Royal Society of Arts made awards to Meigh's firm in that year when it was described as 'one of the most extensive and best-conducted factories of Staffordshire'.

Much of the production was high-quality earthenware, but porcelain was also manufactured, including Parian, and among the firm's outstanding exhibits at the Crystal Palace were a vase and wine cooler in Parian, the vase with classical groups and the wine-cooler elaborately decorated with a Bacchanalian scene. They also exhibited an ambitious clock, in Parian, rather too writhing and coarsely-conceived for modern taste, but highly admired at the time.

Jewitt was enthusiastic in his praise of the Old Hall productions, 'the excellence of the painting, the gilding, the jewelling, and the enamelling, being very apparent in all, and the combination of printing and hand painting carried to great perfection. The transfer-printing at the Old Hall Works is more carefully done, and the colours are clearer and brighter, than at most manufactories. Dessert-services are made in every style of decoration; the richer and more costly varieties being equal to any produced by other firms, both in quality of body, in shape, in pattern, and in artistic treatment'.

Meigh's produced some individual forms of paste which are of technical interest, including 'Indian Stone China', 'Opaque Porcelain', and 'Enamel Porcelain', and they had their own grinding mills for the preparation of 'dry ground' powders for use in both earthenware and china.

The Meigh works, which later assumed the title of 'The Old Hall Porcelain Company', had a most extensive trade in Victorian times, with French, German, American, Indian and Australian connections, so that specimens must still be very numerous in various parts of the world. Here again is a good opportunity for anyone sufficiently interested to bring together a collection of a good, even if not outstanding Victorian firm's work.

MASON'S (IRONSTONE CHINA)

This celebrated ware was manufactured in great quantities during the Victorian era, but the actual invention of it dates back to 1813 when Charles James Mason took out his patent for 'a process for the improvement of the manufacture of English porcelain'.

During its earlier history it was not a commercial success, and in 1851 the patent, together with the expensive moulds and copper plates, passed into the hands of Francis Morley who transferred the manufacture to his own works, having also purchased the business of Hicks, Meigh and Johnson, the only other manufacturers of ironstone china.

Morley thus became the sole proprietor of the ironstone process and he rapidly built it up into a most successful commercial undertaking, gaining a medal for his work at the French Exhibition of 1855. In 1859, however, Morley retired and the process was bought up by the firm of Ashworth whose name is synonymous with the enormous development and popularity of the ware in later times. The title of it has remained 'Mason's Patent Ironstone China' right up to the present and it is still made in large quantities. The durability of 'ironstone china' has made it a firm favourite with clubs, hotels, colleges, liner companies, etc., and the export trade has been vast, services going all over the world.

The name 'ironstone' was a specially happy one, for it at once suggests the essential quality of the ware. The original formula, as specified in the 1813 patent, was 'scoria, or slag of ironstone, pounded and ground in water in certain proportions with flint, Cornwall stone and clay, and blue oxide of cobalt'. Thus the presence of ironstone in the formula may have suggested the name, but whether this was so or not, no title could have been commercially more attractive.

Ashworth's made many beautiful individual objects, besides the popular table-services, including bowls, jugs and vases. Some of the designs are Oriental in inspiration, often with Japanese and Indian floral motifs, the vases and jugs frequently having dragon-shaped handles and in the more expensive pieces richly gilded. Jewitt described some of the 'Indian' vases as 'priceless Art-treasures, and examples of Ashworth's make deserve to be in every "home of taste"'.

Another Victorian firm which made good quality Ironstone China was the Dale Hall works, originally belonging to John and George Rogers, but later acquired by James Edwards and Son. (There was also at Dale Hall the Mayer works, a quite different organization, which is sometimes confused with the Rogers-Edwards firm.)

Some of the Rogers ware has the astrological symbol for Mars (which was intended to symbolize Iron), and the word 'Rogers' as a mark, but the Edwards mark consisted of the Royal Arms with the words 'Stone China, James Edwards and Son, Dale Hall' below, and later a dolphin around an anchor. Later still a circular, then an oval garter with the words 'Ironstone China' was used.

The firm also became very well known for their white granite-ware, and in 1865 received a medal for their electrical and photographic materials in both ironstone china and earthenware.

James Edwards, another character for Arnold Bennett, seems to have had a fascinating personality compounded of benevolence and determination mixed with typically Victorian commercial acumen. He introduced some very progressive machinery into the works when he assumed control in 1842, including 'steam jiggers, lathes, jollies, throwing-wheels, and Needham and Kite's patent pressing machines for preparing clay by filtration'. Edwards was a magistrate of Burslem and before his death distributed a considerable sum of money among his former employees.

Porcelaine Opaque

The collector may from time to time come across individual pieces, and even whole sets, stamped with the words 'Porcelaine Opaque', with the additional word 'Limoges'. This ware, of which the technical name was 'Parisian granite', was made largely by the Anchor Pottery at Fenton, and much of it bears the name of the proprietors, Bridgwood and Son. The New Bridge works at Longport also produced it, though not until after 1877 when Edward Clarke acquired control of the Tunstall Phoenix works and removed them to Longport. A great deal of Clarke's 'porcelaine opaque' was made for export to America and included all kinds of door furniture, finger plates, etc.

'Porcelaine Opaque' was much stronger than ordinary porcelain and had a very tough glaze which made it suitable for such things as artists' palettes and slabs, as well as for the ordinary range of domestic pieces.

ALBERT WORKS (WITH A NOTE ON PARIAN)

The popularity of Parian figures and busts led to many of the smaller factories including them in their catalogues. Some of them made interesting experiments with the Parian body, such as that of the Albert Works (Poole, Stanway and Wood), established in 1859, who decorated the material with majolica colours. They produced a very wide variety of Parian pieces, including groups of figures and single figures, such as the pair 'Night' and 'Morning' by Carrier, and some centre-pieces incorporating groups of female figures, sea-horses, tritons, cupids, etc., with 'elegant open-work dishes' to which the groups gave support.

Another firm, the Wharf Street Works, also at Stoke-on-Trent,

is of particular interest to the collector of Parian for they specialized on it exclusively and probably produced a wider variety of
Parian pieces than any other organization. Their list included such
things as trinket-boxes and bouquet holders as well as the usual
comports and pedestals and jugs. Perhaps their most interesting
series was that of prominent Victorian worthies, including Cob-
den, Tennyson, Dickens, Gladstone, Disraeli, Abraham Lincoln
and Queen Victoria. The very titles of many of their Parian
groups have an unmistakable ring of the Victorian age—'Inno-
cence Protected', 'The Power of Love', 'Guardian Angel', 'Rock
of Ages', etc.

The Wharf Street Works was acquired by Robinson and Leadbeater in 1870, and it was from this date that the extensive manufacture of Parian commenced. Robinson and Leadbeater also
owned the Glebe Street Works at Stoke, having purchased it from
the Italian figure-modeller, Giovanni Meli, who made many
groups and single figures there from its foundation in 1850 till he
sold the works in 1865.

Some idea of the immense popularity of Parian may be obtained
from the fact that one firm, the Trent Pottery at Hanley, which
specialized in the cheaper sort of Parian, produced in a single year
460,000 pieces, many of which went to American and European
markets. Obviously, anyone who wishes to collect 'Victorian
Parian' should have no difficulty in finding supplies since specimens were turned out in such vast quantities.

The variety of subjects, literary, historical, classical, and con-
temporary, was no less astonishing. There were, for instance,
figures and busts of Shakespeare, Milton, Sir Walter Scott,
Cleopatra, Ino and Bacchus, Apollo, Venus, Flora, Theseus and
Diana, The Duke of Wellington, Sir Robert Peel, Jenny Lind,
and the Four Royal Children as the Seasons. The firm of Keys and
Mountford exhibited several pictorial subjects in Parian, such as
'Prometheus Tormented by the Vulture', 'Venus Unrobing at the
Bath', and 'Venus Extracting a Thorn'.

Classical subjects were probably the favourites, but biblical
themes were also popular, for example Minton's 'St Joseph' and

'The Flight into Egypt', 'Naomi and her Daughters in Law', 'The Crucifixion' and 'Christ'. Copelands produced religious pieces too, such as 'The Prodigal Son' and 'Rebecca', and there were a number of vaguely religious groups such as the 'Repentance, Faith and Resignation' exhibited in 1851 by the firm of T. and R. Boote.

Chapter Four

Other Firms: II

WEDGWOOD

THE Wedgwood firm does not enter much into the history of porcelain since the bulk of their famous products has been in earthenware and stoneware. But a little porcelain was made in the early nineteenth century by Wedgwood's nephew, Thomas Byerley, though only for a few years, and porcelain was reintroduced to the Wedgwood programme in 1878, continuing up to the present time.

Some very beautiful work has been produced, often with gilding of high quality, and among the celebrated painters employed was Thomas Allen, who, like Lessore, had been at Mintons before joining Wedgwood.

The porcelain of Wedgwood has been so overshadowed by the firm's other work that it is easy for the collector to overlook it altogether, but much of it is well worth attention. The firm also made attractive deep blue transfer-printed tableware, sometimes with designs of sailing ships against a Mediterranean background, and specimens of these are usually easy enough to acquire though they are not of a true porcellanous texture.

DOULTON

Doulton, like Wedgwood, was not, at all events in the Victorian era, a large porcelain-making firm, but they too, and at about the same time as Wedgwood, introduced the manufacture of porcelain in a special department at their Burslem factory, which had been acquired in 1877. A number of distinguished artists were employed, perhaps the best known being David Dewsberry (his name sometimes appears as Dewsbury) who also achieved distinction in the firm's pottery, especially the 'Carrara' ware.

Doulton porcelain is usually well painted, and the range of subjects includes landscapes, flowers, figures, fish, game, and cattle. The mark is the word 'Doulton', both impressed and printed, the additional word 'England' having been added from about 1891. The initials of the principal artist engaged on the piece are often also to be found.

THE CROWN WORKS

The Crown Works at Burslem, established about 1867, specialized on the manufacture of porcelain 'door furniture' (fingerplates, knobs, and keyhole covers), and some delightful work was done in this all too little appreciated branch of Victorian ceramic art. A small collection of these pieces would be well worth making, as would one of the umbrella, parasol and walking-stick knobs in porcelain which was another speciality of the firm, though other Victorian firms may have made them too. The original proprietors of the Crown Works were Messrs Lea Smith and Boulton, and they were later bought by Messrs Gaskell, Son and Co. Among the firm's many other products in porcelain were caster bowls, lamp stands and bases, and a variety of articles in simulated marble, malachite, and other semi-precious materials.

T. Furnival and Sons, of Stoke, produced good quality Ironstone China, and their dinner-services were often elaborately decorated and gilded. Occasionally sets may be found which show the firm's characteristic blending of hand painting and transfer-printing, together with rich enamelling and gilding. Their toilet-services were also of good quality, being often both elaborate and ingenious, the 'Swan' pattern, for instance, having an oviform ewer of which the neck, mouth and handle were modelled to represent a swan, while the 'Nautilus' service had complex marine decoration, somewhat in the manner of Belleek, with shell, coral and seaweed forms, all carefully modelled on natural growths.

The mark is the word 'Furnival', impressed.

POWELL AND BISHOP

This firm controlled two works in Hanley, one at Stafford Street for the production of high-quality earthenware, and the other, known as the Waterloo Works, for the making of porcelain, though the decoration was all done at the Stafford Street factory.

Their dessert- and tea-services should commend themselves to the collector, especially if he has a taste for richness of detail, since many of them had a form of brilliant gilding resembling an inlay of ormolu, together with fine ground colours and some excellent painting. Powell and Bishop's gilding was much esteemed in Victorian times since it was a patent process which they had bought from an Austrian source and had themselves considerably improved. This process, which produced an effect of rich dead gold, was also used in the firm's fine quality earthenware in which services were made with designs adapted from medieval illuminated manuscripts. This was one of the few instances where the influence of the Gothic Revival can be traced in connection with ceramic art in England.

Beautiful table jugs in porcelain were also made by Powell and Bishop, some of which are in Sèvres blue, also candlesticks and breakfast services.

The firm's work was much praised by contemporary critics and it received medals at the London Exhibition of 1862, at Amsterdam in 1869, and again at Paris in 1875. Their marks were the word 'Best' surmounting the initials P and B, and, later, the same initials over a Caduceus.

MINERVA WORKS, FENTON (AFTERWARDS THE CROWN STAFFORDSHIRE PORCELAIN COMPANY)

These celebrated works were the former home of Charles James Mason and Co., makers of the famous Ironstone China, and, after one or two changes of ownership, they passed into the hands of the Green family. The Greens remained in control throughout the whole of the Victorian period, though in 1890 the firm became a

limited liability company with the title 'The Crown Staffordshire
Porcelain Company'. The earlier work of the firm was not very
distinguished, though their miniature ornaments and toy sets
might perhaps appeal to collectors with restricted accommodation
for their specimens. These were made in large quantities during
the greater part of the Greens' régime, and there must be many
surviving examples. The firm also made trinket services, jugs,
mugs, and some curious 'wheel barrow' and 'spade' salts.

But in the later years of the firm, and particularly from the
inauguration of the Crown Staffordshire Company, some very
interesting reproductions of Chinese styles were made, especially
in vases in *famille verte* and *famille* rose patterns; also some pieces
with floral designs in the manner of Billingsley.

Much careful experimental work was done by the Crown
Staffordshire chemists, and they succeeded in producing several
fine ground colours and enamels, especially a beautiful rose tint
and a very creditable version of the difficult Old English Powder
Blue, which had caused so much trouble to those many manufacturers who had sought to reproduce it.

I recently acquired a fine hexagonal vase by the Crown Staffordshire Company with this powder-blue ground, the panels painted
with birds *à la chinoise* in delicate shades of rose and green. With a
good taste not too common in reproductions of this kind, some of
the porcelain itself is left undecorated, the whole being elegantly
lined in gold, with small floral panels adorning the knopped
cover. The vase very pleasantly suggests the Worcester 'scale
blue and exotic birds' designs, and yet it has its own quality and is
not a slavish copy such as the French firm of Samson so often
turned out.

There was, incidentally, no attempt on the part of the Crown
Staffordshire Company to pass their works off as originals; their
pieces are clearly marked, either with a simple crown, surmounted
with a small cross on a globe, and the word 'Staffs' below (this is
often found on Edwardian pieces) or a more ornate crown above
the word 'Staffordshire' with two interlaced G's as a monogram
underneath.

The firm published their own booklet and explained that they considered their works to be not copies but simply in the tradition of the great porcelain artists of the seventeenth and eighteenth centuries. They had attempted to follow in their path 'with a feeling of reverence and respect', hoping that their productions 'will meet with the appreciation of that large section of the art loving public who wish to preserve in their homes the artistic feeling that seemed to come naturally in the eighteenth century'.

SMALLER FIRMS

It would be impossible in a book of this size to give detailed accounts of all the smaller porcelain factories which sprang up in Victorian England. The Stoke-on-Trent district was particularly prolific of them, and no doubt vast quantities of their pieces are still in existence in various parts of the world, for many of them exported widely as well as carrying on a flourishing trade at home. Some of the ware bore the manufacturer's name or mark, but a great deal of it is anonymous and attribution to its exact place of origin is often now virtually impossible.

Among the host of lesser ceramic planets that circled round the greater constellations, and frequently imitated their styles, many were at Longton and Fenton, and only a small selection of their names can be recorded here:

In Longton there was the firm of Knight and Rowley, whose 'Napier' white and gold tea-service was highly praised by contemporary critics. The Victoria Works produced large quantities of tea-, breakfast- and dessert-services, and also fancy articles of moderate quality. The 'Royal Porcelain Works' (Robinson and Chapman) made good-class services at their model factory which was run by steam power, replacing much of the former manual labour.

Daniel Sutherland and Sons, of Park Hall Street, made a great deal of Parian ware, including brooches and other trinkets, some of their work being marked 'S and S'. The Anchor Pottery

(Sampson, Bridgwood and Sons) made porcelain as well as earthenware, but mostly for American export. They also made 'Parisian Granite' ware, including dessert- and toilet-services, which is stamped 'Limoges', together with the words 'Porcelaine Opaque' and 'Bridgwood and Son'.

Porcelain and 'semi-porcelain' were made by the Dresden Works at Fenton, and by another 'Dresden' factory in Normacott Road. The Fenton Pottery (originally owned by Mason's) produced a characteristic form of ironstone china with embossed patterning; this had a variety of picturesque names, such as the Garland, the Lily, the Missouri, the Florence, and the Versailles. The Fenton Pottery mark was E. and C. Challinor, Fenton, together with a knotted emblem and sometimes the words 'Ironstone China' and the Royal Arms.

The Foley China Works (established in 1850) produced some good quality porcelain. I have a delightful green and gold saucer of theirs, with a triangular central panel, floriated gilt border and central medallion of roses and blue and yellow flowers intermingled, with delicate sprigs of flowers in the angles.

At Tunstall the Greenfield Works made good-class ironstone china which, like that of the Fenton Pottery, had embossed decorative motifs. The Newfield Works, which had family connections with the Greenfield firm, did a flourishing trade with many foreign countries, including Central America, Java, Australia, and the United States.

George Jones's Trent Pottery produced *pâte-sur-pâte* pieces in a somewhat heavy style which compares unfavourably with the Minton masterpieces of Solon, though some of them were well designed, especially those with decorations by F. Schenk.

The firm of Jones was established in 1861 and was well known for its earthenware, white granite and stoneware; it also made majolica ware of good quality, and received awards at Paris in 1867, and again in London in 1871 and Vienna in 1873. The mark is the letters GJ in monogram form.

Left: 33. Copeland plate decorated with ropes and cables surrounding shipping and other scenes. In the centre is the famous steamship, the *Great Eastern*, in its day one of the wonders of the world: sails, as well as the funnels and the paddle wheel, can be seen. The letters GE in monogram are in the spaces between the panels on the border: 1852. *Right:* 34. Plate painted by Arthur Perry with a view of Dinant: Copeland, c. 1850.

Above: 35. Minton teaware and coffee cup with saucer: mazarin blue ground with painted flowers in the white panels: pre-Victorian. *Below:* 36. Copeland tea set with matching tray, showing Indian influence. Decorated in green and gold: 1878.

Left: 37. Pierced coupe shape Minton plate decorated with 'Shrewsbury green' ground; the centre painted by L. Boullemier and signed by him. Raised and chased gold decoration: gold printed mark with word 'England'; Edwardian. *Right:* 38. Copeland plate decorated with gold and flowers and incorporating the monogram of Queen Victoria: c. 1900.

39. Minton vase with cover: mazarin blue ground with oval panels and chased gold ornamentation. Panels in blue and gold; cover in white, gold leafage, gold knob and foot in blue and gold: pre-Victorian.

40. Minton 'Ship' vase (*vaisseau à mât*) with mazarin blue and green ground: exotic birds in panels on each side (probably by L. Boullemier). Gold printed mark with word 'England': used in the Edwardian period.

41. Belleek: ice pail made for the Prince of Wales: mid-Victorian.

42. Minton. Centre piece and vases: mid-Victorian.

43. Minton. Centre pieces and a covered vase: mid-Victorian.

44. Minton. Porcelain clock, thermometer and barometer: mid-Victorian.

45. Copeland vases and ewer: mid-Victorian.

46. Pair of Minton comports: mid-Victorian.

47. Copeland: examples of covered vases: mid-Victorian.

48. Group of Minton vases: mid-Victorian.

49. Four Copeland vases: mid-Victorian.

Top left and below: 50. Worcester ewer and stand painted by Thomas Bott: mid-Victorian. *Top right:* 51. Copeland plate. c. 1840.

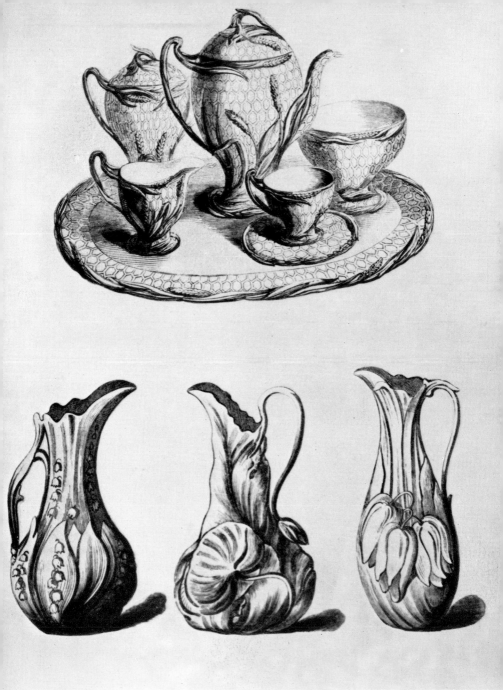

52. Grainger's (Worcester) coffee service 'of very elegant design' with foliage:
also specimens of toilet ware: mid-Victorian.

53. 'Great Porcelain Vase' which was among the Russian exhibits at the Crystal
Palace in 1851: from the official catalogue.

The Hill Top Pottery

This Burslem works had once belonged to Ralph Wood and produced both porcelain and 'semi-porcelain' during the first half of the Victorian era. Samuel Alcock and Co. owned it for some time and later, for a few years, Sir James Duke and Nephews who, however, sold it to 'The Earthenware and Porcelain Company' in 1866.

Some of Sir James Duke's 'Etruscan' vases were notable, and his porcelain generally is worth the collector's attention. The firm afterwards split up into two sections, one for earthenware, one for porcelain, and the porcelain was from 1874 manufactured under the name of Bodley and Son. The usual table-services were made, and some ornamental pans and vases for chandeliers and lamps.

Sir James Duke's mark was a dexter hand, and that of the Alcock régime a beehive.

The Cobridge Works, Burslem

Owned in Victorian times by Messrs Brownfield and Son, this factory attained a very high reputation for its earthenware, and from 1871 the firm also produced porcelain of considerable interest. All the usual services were made, together with centre-pieces, flower stands and vases. Jewitt even described a pair of their vases as 'among the highest achievements of modern Art'.

The firm's work was extensively exported so that pieces may well be encountered very far afield: their trading territories included India, Russia, Australia and New Zealand as well as many European countries.

Sheridan Works, Longton

Is of interest to the student for its intricately decorated pieces made for the Oriental market, notably its little cups and saucers for Morocco, Turkey and Gibraltar, in various Japanese styles, and also 'Japanese' tea-sets, kettles, etc., which were extensively exported to Holland.

F

The works were opened in 1858 by John Sheridan, and were acquired in 1866 by George Edwards and Co.

Harvey Adams and Co.

One of the lesser known Victorian firms, Adams, Scrivener and Co., of Longton, later known as Harvey Adams and Co., produced some fine-quality work which the collector might do well to watch for. This company was a completely Victorian foundation, established at the Sutherland Road Works in 1862. The porcelain itself is good, bearing a beautiful glaze, and a wide range of articles and designs was produced, some of which showed decided originality. For instance, the firm appear to have been the inventors of those very Victorian curiosities, 'moustache cups', afterwards made by many other companies. They also introduced some original forms of porcelain decoration, such as their 'ormolu' effects and the use of silver as a ground. Many of their pieces incorporated silver, used both matt and burnished, sometimes with flowers richly painted over it, and occasionally both silver and gold were employed in the same design.

Jewelled effects, such as 'pearl borders', were another speciality, and many kinds of tea- and dessert-services, with good-quality gilding and enamelling, were made. The firm also became known for its embossed leaf decoration, and services were produced embodying as many as fifty groups of tree and fern foliage designs in relief. These, with characteristic Victorian thoroughness, were carefully copied from the gardens of a Victorian nobleman, the Duke of Sutherland, at Trentham Hall. To give additional variety to the designs they were even reproduced in their spring, summer and autumn colourings; a complete set of these would certainly be well worth purchasing.

Flowers and plants in relief were, in fact, a generic feature of much of Harvey Adams's work, and they appeared on many of their vases and jardinières. Much of their vase and plate painting was of good quality, their best-known artists being Mitchell (animals, figures and landscapes), Swan (flowers), and Longmore (birds).

Chinese, Japanese and Persian designs were produced too, and some of the firm's 'oriental plaques' (such as those painted by Slater, their art manager), would be worth assembling in a collection.

New Town Pottery, Longton

Various owners controlled this factory during the nineteenth century, but during the early years of Victoria's reign it was run by a partnership known as 'Hilditch and Hopwood'. By 1851 they had fully established themselves, and among their products was a lavishly gilt dessert-service with illustrations from Scott's 'Marmion', also tea-services with raised gold foliage, landscape medallions, floral wreaths and good ground colours, including the celebrated Derby blue.

The firm made a speciality of foliage decoration, including geranium leaves, and their general standard of decoration was good, especially their richly burnished gilding and elaborate festoons of roses and other flowers.

The factory was originally in Church Street, but in the latter part of Victoria's reign it was controlled by Messrs Dale, Page and Goodwin, who moved to the 'New Town' works in 1876.

Other Firms

Of the many other factories which had thoroughly established their position by the end of the Victorian era mention may be made of William A. Adderley and Co., H. Aynsley and Co., John Aynsley and Sons, Hammersley and Co., the Longton Porcelain Co., the Stone China Co., Wileman and Co., J. Shore and Co., Edwards and Brown, Hill and Co., Collingwood Bros., the Britannia China Co., the Empire Porcelain Co. (many of their blue and gold vases still turn up at sales), Alfred Meakin, Ltd (the Royal Albert Works), and Charles Allerton and Sons. Allerton's, who were well known for their gold and silver lustre ware which was made right through the Victorian era, also made both 'semi-porcelain' and bone china.

Some good quality porcelain, including Parian, was made by

the firm of William Adams and Son which had been specially famous in the earlier years of the nineteenth century for its fine blue-printed ware with topographical subjects which included a number of American scenes, Niagara Falls, West Point Military School, etc. There were also some beautiful 'London Views' produced at about the same time.

The Adams firm, however, gave up the making of porcelain in 1863 and devoted themselves to high-quality earthenware, though later they produced some 'semi-porcelain' with elaborate Chinese decoration, and also some ironstone china.

Scottish Firms

Scotland enters comparatively little into the general history of English porcelain and in the Victorian era it produced few works of more than passing interest. But, though there was nothing in Scotland comparable with Belleek in Ireland, one or two Scottish firms are worthy of the collector's notice.

The Verreville Pottery, for instance, founded as far back as 1777, began in 1839 to add porcelain to their regular programme of glass and earthenware. (The name 'Verreville' indicates the glass-making origins of the factory, much of which was of very good quality.) R. A. Kidston, who had bought the works in 1835, was the proprietor responsible for branching out into porcelain, and he started in style by engaging artists from Derby, Coalport, and other important centres.

Porcelain, however, was only made for about seventeen years, so that pieces have a certain scarcity value. The quality of the paste was excellent and the range of products included figures, porcelain baskets and porcelain flowers. The Verreville firm seems to have been the first in Scotland to manufacture porcelain; its pieces, therefore, in addition to being scarce, have also an historical value as pioneer work.

This book is concerned with porcelain only, but passing mention may be made here of the Scottish firm of Sprott, Gillespie and Cameron (the Garnkirk Works) which produced many fine pieces of 'garden china', fountains, balustrades, etc., mostly in terracotta and the material known as 'fireclay'. One of their most famous achievements was an enormous public fountain, erected at Aberdeen, five tiers high and adorned with dolphins and cranes, the basin being 24 feet tall and 16 feet across.

The firm had an extensive practice and exported to Europe, Russia and the West Indies.

Another Scottish firm of interest was J. and M. P. Bell and Co. who in 1842 established the Glasgow Pottery, at first for the manufacture of earthenware only, but after 1851 for porcelain also. They produced dinner-, dessert-, tea- and breakfast-services, including some elaborately gilded and enamelled designs. The porcelain was of high quality and the flower painting often very good. The firm also made Parian vases with raised figures.

There is really little else to note in the history of Victorian porcelain in Scotland, but a considerable industry in terracotta and stoneware was built up by various firms besides the one already mentioned. The range of work included garden statuary, flower-stands, ornamental chimney shafts, salt-glazed tiles, finials, pedestals, brackets, plinths, and many other objects.

Finally, anyone interested in collecting teapots might like to note the work of the Alloa Company which in the 1870's was said to be capable of producing 26,000 teapots a week! Some of their better-quality pots were decorated with fernleaf and similar designs and they received medals at Paris and at the Philadelphia Exhibition. Their work was extensively exported and specimens can no doubt still be found widely scattered all over the world, for they traded with Australia, New Zealand, America, Canada, Germany and France.

At the end of the Victorian period a Scottish firm, begun at a small works at Barrowfield, Glasgow, began to make 'Fine Art Ivory Porcelain' which soon expanded into a flourishing business. This was the Nautilus Porcelain Company which produced centre-pieces, tea-sets, dessert-services, figures, vases and trinket sets. Trade developed to such a degree that the firm was able to move to a larger works at the Possil Pottery in northern Glasgow. Here they extended their range to include porcelain baskets with embossed flowers and crest china, this last becoming a very profitable department of the business.

Nautilus porcelain, which was distinguished by a fine ivory tint, was exported to many countries of Europe and also to the British Colonies and to America.

Chapter Five

Pattern Numbers, Cyphers and Registration Marks

THE dating of Victorian porcelain is helped in many cases by the pattern numbers and cyphers used by the principal firms, and by the Registration Marks printed on pieces between the years 1842 and 1883.

Pattern numbers, however, can be misleading unless it is remembered that they only indicate the date at which the pattern was first put into circulation, and this may not be the date of the actual piece in hand. But they do show definitely that a piece could not be earlier than the date at which the pattern number was introduced.

The usual method of numbering patterns was to proceed up to 9999 and then either start again with a prefixed letter or to place a numeral over the pattern number to show that it belonged to a fresh series or book. Copelands, for instance, used the letter system until about 1852 when, on reaching 9999, a D was prefixed to the new numbers. When the D series had also reached 9999, towards 1880, the prefix 1/ was added which went on until early in the twentieth century.

Coalport also used a letter-prefix system, but with a classification for various groups, V for vases, X and Z for dinner- and dessert-services, and Y for tea-services. They had size prefixes too, S/s for small, M/s for middle and L/s for large; their pattern numbers remained below 5000 during the Victorian period.

Derby pieces, however, do not usually have pattern numbers at all until the founding of the new Derby works in 1876 when an ordinary numerical system was adopted, proceeding up to about 6000 by the end of the Victorian epoch.

Minton numbering was somewhat more complicated, and the firm used an elaborate cypher system by which not only the year of manufacture, but the actual month can be determined. This began in 1842 and went on into the present century. In addition to the cyphers the letter-prefix system was used, beginning in 1850 with A and being succeeded in 1868 by G. This went on until the end of the century, though other letters were used as well, for instance, 'O' for ornaments and 'P' and 'P A' for the more costly ware.

Worcester dating is also somewhat complicated although the actual marks, which changed every few years until 1867, help to date the earlier Victorian pieces fairly closely. There were the various Chamberlain marks up to 1852, the Kerr and Binns marks up to 1867, and then the rare 'Crowned W' mark of 1862–1870. (approx.)

From 1867, however, dating is fixed by the letter system, ranging from A in 1867 to Z in 1888, O being omitted and then used in 1889. F, Q and J were omitted altogether and a small 'a' used in 1890. After this a dot system was adopted, the dots occurring over the lettering of 'Royal Worcester England'; by counting these dots, beginning with one in 1892, the pieces of the end of the century and the Edwardian age can be pinned down to their precise year.

Worcester used pattern numbers as well, going on into the 9,000's with no prefix up to about 1878. B was then used as a prefix, but only for a short time, and from 1880 to the end of the century the prefix was W.

The Grainger works used a letter system of marking, though this did not begin until roughly 1890.

Many pieces of Victorian porcelain are stamped with a diamond-shaped Registration Mark containing the letters Rd. This was a device used between 1842 and 1883 and indicated that the design was registered at the Patent Office and therefore could not be copied in any form. The marks inside the diamond were of two kinds, the first in operation from 1842 to 1867, the second from 1868 to 1883. A to Z in the top angle of the diamond represents the year date between 1842 and 1867, and A to Y in the right-hand angle the year from 1868 to 1883.

It should be noted, however, that the letters were not used consecutively, the actual sequence being as follows:

Year Mark at top:
A, 1845. B, 1858. C, 1844. D, 1852. E, 1855. F, 1847. G, 1863. H, 1843. I, 1846. J, 1854. K, 1857. L, 1856. M, 1859. N, 1864. O, 1862. P, 1851. Q, 1866. R, 1861. S, 1849. T, 1867. U, 1848. V, 1850. W, 1865. X, 1842. Y, 1853. Z, 1860.

Year Mark in right-hand angle:
A, 1871. C, 1870. D, 1878. E, 1881. F, 1873. H, 1869. I, 1872. J, 1880. K, 1883. L, 1882. P, 1877. S, 1875. U, 1874. V, 1876. W (March 1–6 only), 1878. X, 1868. Y, 1879.

From 1884 to 1901 an ordinary numerical system was used, beginning at 1 and reaching 368,154 by 1901 (i.e. roughly 20,000 per year).

Chapter Six

Conclusion

IT IS still too early to estimate the final place which Victorian Porcelain will take in the esteem of connoisseurs and collectors. Like the arts of the Victorian age as a whole, it is likely to have both its defenders and its detractors for some considerable time to come. Certainly it can never hope to have the 'pioneer' appeal of Bow or Chelsea nor can its most sumptuous achievements compete with the great masterpieces of Sèvres and Meissen as heirlooms from a civilization of perfect taste. For the Victorian age was far from being an age of perfect taste. It was, on the contrary, a tumultuous time in which so many conflicting tendencies and claims clamoured for expression that it is difficult for even the most devoted student of it to see it steadily and see it whole. It was the age, for instance, of figures and movements so widely diverse as the pre-Raphaelites and the great railway engineers, of the workhouse horrors chronicled by Dickens and of the saintliness of Cardinal Newman and the Tractarians, of the heavy literary splendours of Ruskin and of the elegant playfulness of Oscar Wilde.

Its architecture ranged from the brilliance of Barry and Pugin to the tawdriness of many of its villas and the plutonian gloom of many of its factories and slums. There were superb buildings like Waddesdon Manor; there were the back to back terraces of Leeds and Nottingham.

And similarly with the porcelain of the period. There were the magnificent works of the great factories, their great dinner-services and splendidly ornate vases, their exquisite candelabra and pierced porcelain baskets, their elegant Parian figures, their beautiful tazzas and coffee-cups and flower-stands and *jardinières*. At the other extreme were the frightful cheap bedroom ornaments and some of the brash table-services, many poorly designed and abominably executed figurines, china children of unbearable ugliness and teapots of nightmare nastiness.

Between these extremes lay an infinite gradation of styles and levels of taste and quality. And unfortunately one too often encounters Victorian pieces in which some of the features will be perfectly satisfactory, such as the gilding or the modelling, only to be spoiled by other features badly conceived and badly carried out. For this reason the collector may sometimes find it difficult to make up his mind whether he thinks a piece has been put outside the pale by some inherent ineptitude, or whether its redeeming features are good enough to justify adding it to his collection.

All that can be said by way of general advice is that the more one studies and steeps oneself in the Victorian age the wider one's appreciation of its idiosyncrasies and toleration of its many weaknesses will become. And though the aphorism *comprendre tout, c'est tout pardonner* cannot ever apply to everything the Victorians produced, yet it remains true that one does learn to enjoy a great deal of the more 'difficult' Victoriana as one's knowlege of the period grows.

A criticism of Victorian porcelain that is frequently heard is that it was, like the other arts of the age, fundamentally backward-looking, that it did not advance ceramic art but imprisoned it in the strait-jacket of historicism and reproduction of past glories. Our own age has cast off the shackles of the past so violently, in the arts, in political ideas, in education and in scientific thought, that we are now out of sympathy with historicism in any form as a standard or as a guide.

But it has always to be remembered that much of the greatest art of the past was itself inspired by that of former times. Shakespeare's plays provide a striking instance of this since almost all of them have themes taken from the past, classical antiquity, medieval or Renaissance stories, and ancient British history. Again, the great glories of Renaissance and Baroque architecture, such as St Peter's in Rome and St Paul's in London, are very strongly influenced by classical models and even reproduce many classical features, yet no one is ever heard to criticize them as artistically shallow or backward-looking or sterile or unprogressive.

It is, therefore, unfair to dismiss some of the truly lovely works of the Victorian ceramic artists as unworthy of serious attention merely because they fall into line with the generally accepted artistic canons of their century. Almost all the great men of the nineteenth century, not only in England but in the whole of Europe, were deeply interested in the past and strove to continue its traditions rather than to break with them; the porcelain artists of the time were no exception.

But what the collector will find of most absorbing interest and value is to distinguish between the work which was merely reproductive and that which was traditional yet individual. Certainly the greater achievements of Victorian porcelain, such as the masterpieces of Solon produced at Mintons, are well worthy of a place alongside the splendours of the Golden Age of porcelain. For while continuing the traditions of the past they are also experimental and progressive and are at the same time thoroughly imbued with the feeling and character of the age from which they sprang.

Appendix A

Porcelain Artists of the Victorian Period

PRINCIPAL ARTISTS

THE collector will find it valuable to know the names of the principal artists who worked for the greater firms during the Victorian period, their place of employment, and the subjects on which they specialized. The following list, which does not aim at being more than a representative selection, will show under the four convenient headings of Flowers, Birds, Landscapes and Figures, the best-known artists in each group, although there is some overlapping since only a few artists specialized exclusively on any one subject.

Under the heading of figures are included a few of the more famous modellers and here also will be found some of the celebrated general ceramic artists of the time who are not listed under other headings, such as M. L. Solon and James Hadley.

Artists occasionally moved from one works to another, in which case they will appear under their various factories; sometimes a father and son of the same name worked in succession at the same factory, and it is not then always possible for even the most expert eye to differentiate their work.

FLOWERS

Mintons:
Bancroft, Joseph	Kirkby, Thomas
Coleman, Helen	Latham, John
Cooper, Wm.	Leroy, Désiré
Dudley, M.	Mussill, W.
Green, Aaron	Penson, Henry
Gregory, A.	Pilsbury, Richard

Randall, G.
Reuter, E. G.
Rivers, L.
Simpson, T. H.
Slater, Albert
Smith, Jesse

Steele, Edwin
Steele, Thomas
Stewart, R.
Walklett, R.
Wareham, Joseph

Copelands: Adams, F. W.
Arrowsmith, John
Bancroft, Joseph
Brough, Charles
Cartlidge, John

Dean, J.
Hürten, C. F.
Lee, Harry
Sadler, T.
Smith, J.

Coalport: Aston, Jabez
Birbeck, Joseph
Bowdler, Arthur
Cook, William
Dixon, Thomas
Eaton, R.
Jones, Cecil

Latham, John
Parker, John,
Pattern, Josiah
Rouse, James
Stephens, Hamlet
Trevies, William
Williams, John

Derby: Gregory, A.
Lead, Leonard
Leroy, Désiré

Steele, Horatio
Wale, John

Worcester: Bates, David
Evans, David (Grainger's)
Locke, Edward
Phillips, E.

Raby, Edward
Sherriff, James
(also son of same name)
Taylor, William

Brown-Westhead, Moore:
Edwards, Thomas
Leonce, G.

Mallet, P.

Davenport: Eaton, R.

BIRDS

Mintons: Bayley, E. S.
Birbeck, William
Heath, C.
Leroy, Désiré
Mitchell, Henry

Mussill, W.
Randall, G.
Wareham, Joseph
Wright, Albert

Copelands: Arrowsmith, John
Brough, Charles
Lee, Harry

Weaver, James
Weaver, Charles

Coalport: Birbeck, Joseph
Parker, John

Randall, John
Williams, John

Derby: Leroy, Désiré

Worcester: Baldwyn, C. H.
Hopewell, John

Powell, William
Weaver, James

Brown-Westhead, Moore:
Leonce, G.

LANDSCAPES

Mintons: Evans, John
Green, Aaron

Pratt, H. L.

Copelands: Birbeck, William
Lucas, Daniel, Jr.

Perry, Arthur
Yale, W.

Coalport: Ablott, Richard
Ball, E. O.
Birbeck, William
Hall, Arnold
Harper, John

Lucas, Daniel
Mountford, Jesse
Plant, J. H.
Steele, Thomas, Jr.

Derby: Ablott, Richard   Prince, Edward
            Dean, W. E.   Rouse, James
            Hancock, H. S.   (also son of same name)
            Holtzendorf, Count   Wale, John

Worcester: Doe, Enoch   Stinton, John
             Perling, Robert   Williams, Joseph

Brown-Westhead, Moore:
            Ellis, Joseph

Davenport: Mountford, Jesse

FIGURES
(including some of the more celebrated modellers)

Mintons: Allen, Thomas   Longmore, Thomas
            Bell, John (Modeller)   (Modeller)
            Birks, A.   Protât, H. (Modeller)
            Birks, L. A.   Reuter, E. G.
            Boullemier, Anton   Rischgitz, Edouard
            Carrier de Belleuse, Albert Roberts, Ellis
            Cocker, George   Rouchard, François
            Coleman, Rebecca   Simpson, John
            Eyre, George   Solon, L. V.
            Foster, H. W.   Solon, M. L.
            Heath, C.   Thomas, John
            Henk, John   (Modeller)
            Jahn, Louis   Turner, Alice
            Jeannest, Emile
            Kirkby, Thomas
            Lessore, Emile
               (afterwards did distin-
               guished work at Wedg-
               woods)

Copelands:	Abraham, R. F. Alcock, Samuel	Besche, L. Gibson, John (Modeller)
Coalport:	Abraham, R. F. Hartshorne, J.	Palmore, Charles Rouse, James
Derby:	Cocker, George (Modeller) Haslem, John	Landgraff, G. Platts, James
Davenport:	Fletcher, W.	
Worcester:	Bott, Thomas Callowhill, James Callowhill, Thomas Doe, Enoch (also son of same name) Evans, George (Modeller) Hadley, James (Modeller)	Kirk, W. B. Owen, George Palmere, Charles Rushton, Josiah Sutton, F. Toft, Charles

Appendix B

Marks

THERE are a number of excellent dictionaries and hand-lists of Manufacturers' Marks now available to the collector and reference should be made for more detailed information to some of these. Outstanding among recent works is Mr Geoffrey Godden's fine 'Encyclopaedia of British Pottery and Porcelain Marks" (1964).

The following short list, however, covers the principal marks of the major firms referred to in this book, though it does not pretend to be exhaustive, and, as has been already indicated, marks on Victorian porcelain are a perfectly reliable source for establishing the authenticity of specimens since so far there has been no purpose in producing spurious Victorian pieces for commercial profit. Even so, much quite good-quality work was made in the Victorian period itself which set out, more or less deliberately, to ape the highly priced porcelain of the great factories, such as Worcester and Derby, and care may sometimes be needed to distinguish this from genuine examples. Generally, if the pieces offered to the collector bear no mark but are clearly in the style of the greater firms they are unlikely to be genuine since most of their work was definitely marked. However, this rule cannot be too constantly applied since, for instance, some of the most beautiful Sèvres-style plates produced by Coalport during the mid-century have no mark of any kind.

It should be noted that, in addition to the main marks, some manufacturers, such as Mintons, Derby and Worcester, adopted an elaborate cypher system for dating, and it is possible, with the help of this, as well as with the diamond-shaped Registration Marks in use from 1842 to 1883, to pin many pieces down to their particular year and even their particular months of manufacture. This is a pursuit with its own niceties of detective-tracking, as with the six numbered swans on Minton ware from 1895 to 1900 and the elaborate system of dots on Worcester pieces from 1892 onwards.

MINTON

'Ermine' mark, used *circa* 1850.

Exhibition mark used, *circa* 1860–70.

Mark used for some ten years from *circa* 1863; the London retailers' names appeared in the 'ribbons'.

Crown and globe mark with 's' appended to 'Minton'; used in the 1870's. The word 'England' was added *circa* 1890.

COPELAND

Used 1847–67

Used 1847–c. 1850

The same mark but in a more elaborate form, Used c. 1850–85.

COPELAND

Used 1875–90.

Used at the extreme end of the Victorian period; *circa* 1894 onward.

COALPORT

Much Coalport ware is unmarked though imitation Sèvres, Chelsea and Meissen marks occur in the 1840's and 1850's.

 Crown mark used 1881–91.

The same mark with the word 'England' added 1891 onwards.

BELLEEK

WORCESTER

 Chamberlain mark, 1850–52.

 Kerr and Binns mark, 1852–62.

 Shield mark, with year of the century (last two numbers only) in space at right. Kerr and Binns period.

 Used in the 1860's.

 Crown added to the earlier Kerr and Binns mark from 1862. The last two numbers of the year of the century will be found at the bottom of the circle.

 'Royal Worcester, England' added from 1891, together with a dot-dating system. Every extra dot indicates a year from 1891.

 Hadley mark, 1896–7.

Later Hadley mark, 1897–1900.

 Edwardian Hadley mark, 1902–5.

DERBY

 Early Bloor mark, *circa*, 1820–40.

Later Bloor mark, *circa* 1830–48.

 Imitation Sèvres mark used by Bloor.

Mark used by Locker and Co. who succeeded Bloor.

 Stevenson and Hancock mark. Used from *circa* 1862 onwards.

Crown Derby mark, with the addition of the word 'Royal' from 1890 when the Royal warrant was issued.

DAVENPORT

 Anchor mark, used 1850–70.

Later Davenport mark, used 1870–80.

BERNARD MOORE

 Used from 1880.

BELL'S OF GLASGOW

One of several marks used. Others include a simple 'bell' mark, without the surrounding belt.

COBRIDGE

BOOTH'S

17 50 'Silicon China' mark.

CAULDON PLACE

Ridgway mark. Other marks included 'J.W.R.' in a shield, and 'Ridgway and Sons'.

I. RIDGWAY

MEIGH'S (OLD HALL)

One of several Meigh marks. Others included the words 'Opaque Porcelain' and 'Enamel Porcelain'. Also the word 'Meigh'.

ROCKINGHAM

One of several Rockingham marks.

ROYAL ROCKINGHAM
BRAMELD

MASON'S

Variants of this mark occur, e.g. with the name 'Ashworth' added below.

T. AND R. BOOTE

Ironstone china mark.

ROYAL   PATENT
IRONSTONE
T & R BOOTE

CROWN STAFFORDSHIRE

One of several marks. Occurs on Edwardian pieces.

Appendix C

The Great Exhibition of 1851

T H E following is a selection of the most interesting exhibits of the principal firms in the department of the Exhibition which was devoted to 'China, Porcelain, Earthenware, etc.'. This formed Class 25 of Section III and was shown in the North Transept Gallery. There were sixty-two exhibitors in all, though this did not include the foreign porcelain displays, such as those of Sèvres and St Petersburg, which appeared under the auspices of their own country's stands.

Mintons and Copelands were by far the largest of the English porcelain exhibitors, many of the other firms showing only a few articles, though Wedgwood made an extensive display of their famous earthenware and stoneware.

In this selection the spelling and phrasing of the 1851 Catalogue have been preserved, including the hyphenated 'or-molu', 'marone' and the constantly misnamed 'Rose du Barry'. The list of items was attractively punctuated with explanatory comments on various technical processes which are of great interest as they show exactly what contemporary methods of production were.

MINTON'S

Dessert-Service, consisting of assiettes montées, round, oval, and triangular baskets, jelly stands, wine coolers, cream bowls, salt cellars, elevated and low comports, perforated china, in turquoise and gold, painted Cupids, flowers and fruit, with Parian figure and ornamental supports; ornaments, gilt and chased, and candlesticks in Parian, gilt, and plates of various patterns.

Porcelain Vases. Large vase, with perforated ornaments, decorated and finished with or-molu mountings.

Pair of Parnassus vases, being a combination of china and Parian; the china in mazarine and gold, and the bas-relief, Apollo and the Muses, in Parian.

Vases, a pair, bleu de roi, and a pair Sèvres green; the grounds, with painted flowers, and raised festoons, gilt.

Pair of egg-form vases, turquoise ribbons, painted wreaths of flowers and laurel on one side: groups of flowers on the reverse, and gilt.

Pair of rope festoon vases, Sèvres green ground, painted festoons of oak and laurel, and wreaths of flowers, bird in compartment, and gilt.

Inkstand, Sèvres green cross-bars, painted wreaths of flowers, and gilt.

Pair of seaux, turquoise diamonds, painted birds in compartments, and roses in small compartments, and gilt.

Pair of candlesticks with figures in the costume of the time of Louis XV.

Parian Figures: Statuettes: 'Dorothea', 'Miranda', 'Clorinda', 'Una and the Lion', 'Triton and Nautilus', the 'Babes in the Wood', by John Bell. 'The Infant Neptune', by H. J. Townsend. 'The Distressed Mother'; from the statue by Sir R. Westmacott; 'Cupid indignant', with pedestal, and festoons of raised flowers; 'Temperance', Flora.

Mercury (after Thorwaldsen); *Shakespeare,* by John Bell; *Sir Robert Peel; The Prince of Wales.*

Set of Chessmen, by John Bell. *Chimney piece* in Parian. *Ewers* with stands, after Cellini.

Vases, with embossed festoons and ornaments, gilt. Roman Cippus vases, embossed birds and foliage, and turquoise ground.

Group of raised flowers, with a Cupid in the centre, and a twisted dolphin support.

COPELAND'S

Works in Porcelain statuary: Group of Ino and the Infant Bacchus; 'Paul and Virginia'; Sir Robert Peel, Jenny Lind, Duke of Wellington. 'The Return from the Vintage'.

A vase of Etruscan form, with chased and burnished gold ornaments, on a blue ground, decorated with floral wreaths, enamelled, in colours, &c, with pedestal 40 inches high.

The Dove Tazza, and pedestal. The birds and embossments in solid gold, chased, turquoise ground, and floral wreath, &c. Another with royal blue grounds, the details of ornament in gold and silver.

Pair of vases, rose ground, chased gold panels, with musical emblems and flowers.

Warwick vase, 24 inches high, and 28 inches wide, royal blue ground, in chased and burnished gold.

Circular plateau for table (fine porcelain), turquoise grounds, gold ornaments, chased and burnished, with vignettes of flowers, Watteau subjects, &c.

Porcelain table, cyclamon ground (new tint), with chased gold panels, Watteau vignettes and wreaths and groups of flowers. Another, with borders in chased and burnished gold, on blue ground, and festoons of convolvulus.

Dessert plates with scroll borders in chased and burnished gold on a blue ground; in the inner and outer borders the royal initials and coronet are introduced; and the royal arms in the centre.

A jewel design on cyclamon ground (double tint), emblazoned in enamels and gold, with the arms of His Grace the Duke of Sutherland. A crimson ground, containing the arms of His Grace the Duke of Wellington. Cyclamon ground, with the arms of His Grace the Duke of Devonshire.

Specimens of Gothic pierced plates, with a chased gold border, and a wreath of blossoms and fruit in the centre.

Two wedding plateaux for supporting a bride cake; containing appropriate mottoes and entwining wreaths of orange blossom and passiflora.

Another plateau with an enamelled and gilt wreath of orange blossom and passiflora of the natural size.

MASON'S

Specimens of patent ironstone china.

Garden seats of a mixed Anglo-Indian and Japanese pattern, representing an old dragon, in raised enamel on a gold ground.

Jars with raised enamel Mandarin figures, and sea-dragon handles.

Jugs of old Indian, Japanese, and gold patterns, of the original shape; also Anglo-Indian and melon pattern; with oriental figures and gold ornaments. Ewer and basin, and mouth ewer and basin, with oriental figures and a rose border.

Red and gold paint jars. Zig-zag beakers, on bronze. Table-ware of a Japanese pattern in blue, red and gold.

RIDGWAYS

Tea- and coffee-service, azure and gold, with gold star.

Table-service, British wild flowers, Dresden style; border, embossed and gold.

Lawn fountain, white and gold, playing. Conservatory fountains for playing.

WEDGWOOD'S

In addition to their large exhibition of earthenware, Wedgwood's showed some 'Carrara statuary porcelain' which included 'figures from the antique' such as Venus and Cupid, Hercules, Morpheus, and 'Fawn with flute'.

MEIGH'S

A porcelain ornamented candlestick. Vases: pink grounds, flowers and gold, chased; Celeste ground, chased gold. The Murder of the Innocents; pair, Cleopatra and Anne Boleyn, marone grounds, chased gold. Large vases with portraits of the Queen and view of the Exhibition Building; and of Prince Albert, with interior view. Large stork vase, with water birds painted on each side.

Clock, subject 'Night and Morning', with a figure of Silence on the top.

BOOTE'S

Statuettes in Parian, about 20 inches high, Shakespeare, Milton, Venus, &c.

Parian bust of Sir Robert Peel, taken from the picture by Sir Thomas Lawrence.

HILDITCH AND HOPWOOD

Centre-piece on pillar, with embossed vine border; grapes suspended.

BRAMELD (i.e. ROCKINGHAM)

Ice pail of Rockingham china, gilt, with enamel painting of 'Birdtrap' and 'Charity', with snow scenes, on the foot, and stem of green holly and berries.

Grape basket, with Guava cup for pine apple, and wreath of gilded union flowers in china.

Breakfast cup and saucer of the original Rockingham glaze, painted with flowers, and the rose, shamrock, and thistle, gilt.

CHAMBERLAIN'S (WORCESTER)

Tea-service of egg-shell china, with a medallion of Shakespeare on each cup.

Communion and déjeûne services, of pierced or honey-comb china.

Portfolio china slabs, with view of Malvern, and scene from 'Twelfth Night'.

Adelaide vases, gilt, &c., with views of Constantinople and Smyrna, and paintings of various kinds.

Snake-handle vases, with views of Worcester and Malvern. Coventry vases with medallions of Shakespeare and Milton.

Gold and white Dresden baskets, with paintings.

JOHN ROSE AND CO. (COALPORT)

Dessert-services, Rose du Barry, raised gold and flowers. Embossed dessert-services, green and gold, with plants, enamelled. Embossed services, Celeste, gold and birds.

Tea-services—roses in gold ground, Victoria green and gold, turquoise ground and gold border, and white and gold.
Tripod epergne, with pierced basket, Cupids, in Parian, representing the Seasons. Smaller epergne, supported by sea-horses, in Parian.

Flower-vases, turquoise and gold, supported by dolphins; also, solid gold chased. Lamp-pillar, pink and gold.

Small coffee sets, Rose du Barry, gold, &c. Celeste, gold, &c.
Clock-case, gilt, with figures of Time and Cupid (Parian). Group of figures: 'Puck and companions' (Parian).

And as a curiosity: (exhibited by *James Green*)

'Papworth's registered fountain, manufactured in china or earthenware, for large saloons and conservatories, supplied by the high-water services. It can be more easily kept clean than other material, and, being capable of a great variety of colours, is ornamental in an apartment. It is also conducive to health, by preventing undue dryness of air from heating apparatus.'

THE CRYSTAL PALACE EXHIBITS. A CONTEMPORARY CRITICISM

The *Art Journal* of 1851 offered a prize, which was won by R. N. Wornum, for the best essay on the way in which the Crystal Palace Exhibition could be made most useful to British manufacturers of porcelain. This winning essay contains many revealing comments which show clearly that mere imitation of the past glories of porcelain was severely frowned on by contemporary connoisseurs. And yet the strongly developed historical sense which underlay Victorian art as a whole emerges from all the writer's strictures on slavish copying, and he himself holds up the

Greek ceramic forms as the best ideals for modern potters to follow:

'Repudiate the idea of copying as we will, all our vagaries end in a recurrence to Greek shapes. All the most beautiful forms in the Exhibition, whether in silver, in bronze, in earthenware, or in glass, are Greek shapes; it is true, often disfigured by the accessory decorations of the modern style, but still Greek in their essential form.' He goes on to praise the Copeland exhibits whose variation of classical models 'appears to us to constitute the true use of these ancient remains, and the best evidence of a refined taste'.

It is, in fact, quite clear that most of the exhibits at the Crystal Palace were fundamentally imitative of past styles, with 'Indian, Moorish and Cinquecento' styles, as well as many examples in the manner of Sèvres. 'The Louis Quinze,' says Wornum, 'is still the prevailing style, in porcelain as in many other manufactures; and, generally speaking, profusion of ornament is the rule.' There follows a detailed account of the sumptuous display of Mintons, including a dessert-service in turquoise, white and gold, purchased by Queen Victoria herself, which Wornum criticized as having Louis Quinze details in too conspicuous profusion. He describes also a pair of vases with metal handles elaborately detailed with ram's head, scroll, cornucopia and putti decoration, and some avowed imitations of old Dresden and 'the school of Watteau'.

Wornum was plainly himself possessed of a considerably purer taste than some of the manufacturers. Besides criticizing the too frequent profusion of ornament he stressed the importance of ceramic form which 'should command the first consideration; a vessel, even should it have no other attraction than an agreeable shape, or, in other words, be wholly without decoration, may still be a beautiful and delightful object to the cultivated eye, and will itself eventually educate the uncultivated. Shape is the element of beauty; decoration may enhance it, if judiciously applied, and may do much towards destroying it if had recourse to in too great proportion; but it is this, more or less, which tests the quality of taste'.

These were words of excellent advice, and seem to point

surprisingly towards the artistic canons of the twentieth century, but it cannot be said that the porcelain manufacturers of the time took much notice of them. For profusion of ornament, often applied to ugly and awkward forms, continued to be the ruling principle of porcelain manufacture for many years to come. There was, however, a laudable desire by a number of firms to extend the whole territory of porcelain, and pottery too, to objects which it had never before embraced. And though this led to some unbelievable absurdities, such as 'ceramic stair-rails' and some of those hideous encaustic tiles which disfigured the floors of so many Victorian churches, the movement as a whole was on the right lines.

The remarkable development of the ceramic tile industry, for example, while producing some horrors, helped considerably to break down the dominance of past styles since it called by its very nature for some fresh thinking in design and technique. In many of the charming fireplace and overmantel designs, and in some of the schemes for lining corridor and passage walls in public buildings, theatres, town halls, hotels, etc., there was a definite originality displayed.

Appendix D

The Manufacture of Porcelain

THE making of porcelain is dependent on the supply of Kaolin, or china-clay, and petuntse, or china-stone, both of which have been in England largely obtained from Cornwall and Devon. Kaolin has come from the various Cornish-clay districts, including St Austell and St Stephens, and also from the Devonshire district of Lee Moor.

It is essential, in the preparation of Kaolin, to have a good natural water supply and to find rock in which the felspar has decomposed so that it is in a state of disintegration. This is necessary because the quartz, schorl, mica and other minerals in the rock are extracted by a system of washing, leaving the decomposed felspar in a soft clay-like paste to be collected in tanks and then sufficiently dried to be marshalled in the form of lumps for transport direct to the various pottery towns.

China-stone, which has also come largely from Cornwall, is of different kinds, normally a compound of quartz and felspar, but always with a proportion of alkaline silicate so that the material is fusible enough to be converted into a paste for the making of porcelain. The presence of minerals such as schorl or black tourmaline has to be watched for, and any strong admixture of iron specially avoided since it would colour the paste of which the porcelain has to be made. China-stone, unlike Kaolin, can be transported in its natural state to the factories, being merely split up into smaller pieces for the purposes of transit and, on arrival at the works, ground into powder.

In addition to Kaolin and china-stone, natural clay, such as that found in Devon and Dorset, has been widely used, though often a proportion of the prepared Kaolin from Cornwall has been added, according to the type of paste ultimately required. Silica in the form of a creamy substance could then be added to the body of the material and artificially combined with it to give the necessary fusibility.

The general processes of manufacture of both earthenware and porcelain are similar, and this, of course, explains why so many firms have made both kinds. The differences are largely due to the way in which the various pastes are compounded, to the kinds of kiln which have to be employed, and to the differing glazes. 'Muffle kilns', for instance, have always been essential for the firing of enamel colours on porcelain; in these a form of artificial protection from the great heat is given to the articles.

The pastes themselves have varied a great deal in the proportion of their components. At the beginning of the Victorian era the proportion was roughly 30 per cent of Cornish clay, 25 per cent of Cornish stone, 40 per cent of prepared bone, and a little flint, the bone ash being the famous English ingredient introduced by Spode, though others had earlier experimented with it. These proportions, however, were varied considerably in the course of the nineteenth century, and there was also much variety in the kinds of glaze employed. Glazes were made of varying compounds of felspar, gypsum, borax, salt, potash, soda, and oxide of lead, the coloured glazes being made by adding oxides of metals such as cobalt, iron and manganese. Lead glaze was a specially dangerous form to use and felspathic glazes (i.e. with a strong proportion of felspar) were experimented with, as at Coalport as early as 1820.

The colouring ingredients for porcelain have to be combined with a flux, which will vitrify when fused with the body of the article and provide the double service of fixing the colours to the paste and of glazing them over. The colourings formed are then applied, but owing to the intense heat of the firing-kilns which tends to distort the chromatic effects desired only a limited number of under-glaze colours can be produced in such a way as to be relied on. Cobalt will produce not only blue, but also black and grey; manganese gives violet and black, iron peroxide red, brown, and violet, oxide of antimony yellow, and chromium green.

The use of special muffle-kilns is essential for the enamelling and gilding processes, which are of great delicacy and require specialized skill for proper results. Gilding is produced by a mixture of gold powder and mercury, together with turpentine and oil which is applied to the piece, the whole being then put into the muffle-kiln for firing. When it is withdrawn it will be in the form of 'dead gold' which, if a brilliant effect is required, can then be brought to a high state of brilliance by the burnishing process. The raised gold decoration which appears on many of the more expensive works is produced by the application of enamel tracing before the gold is first applied; this provides a raised groundwork which makes the gilding stand out from the surface of the porcelain.

The actual processes of production of the finished porcelain paste from the raw materials of Kaolin and china-stone were described by a number of Victorian writers, and the following account has been based entirely on contemporary sources; the reader will, of course, realize that a number of these processes have now been considerably modified by modern methods:

The principal ingredients, Kaolin, china-stone, prepared bone and flint, are mixed in the proportion required and water added so that the whole is in a heavy liquid form. The mixture is then taken to the slip-kiln, a trough made of brick and heated by flues. When the paste has become like dough it is taken out and stored in cold cellars till it is needed. Metal oxides can be added to the mixture at this stage if the paste is required to be tinted in any way.

When the process of shaping begins the prepared paste is 'thrown' on a potter's wheel which produces, together with the action of the human hand, the various elementary shapes required. Plaster of Paris moulds are also used, into which the paste can be pressed, having first been rolled into convenient pieces. The next stage is the drying of the finished shapes, since they will all still contain an amount of moisture. When they are dried they are carefully packed into 'saggers' (the word may be a corruption of 'safeguard') and taken to the 'biscuit kiln' where they are subjected to intense heat for several days. On being withdrawn the articles are then said to be in the 'biscuit' stage and are ready for the application of paint or transfer printing. If the decoration is to be 'under-glaze' it is now applied, though, as indicated above, only a limited range of colours can be employed since the glaze itself will also have to be fired to fix it on to the paste. But if the decoration is 'over-glaze' (i.e. enamel colours or gilding) a wider range of colours can be used because these will not be added until the piece emerges from the 'glost oven'. This is the oven for glazing to which everything is taken for a second firing after it has been dipped in whatever kind of glaze is being used.

Transfer-printing requires great care and dexterity, especially in the removal of the transfer-paper so that the design is not damaged in any way. The oil still left on the decoration is expressed by placing the pieces in a low-heated kiln.

When the glaze, which is in liquid form, has been applied to the articles by dipping them carefully into a vat of it, and when they have been through the glost oven they will be ready for any over-glaze decoration which is required, and then taken to a muffle-kiln for their final firing.

Owing to the contraction of all forms of ceramic paste, both for porcelain and earthenware, under the great heat of the kilns, it is necessary to allow for this in the original modelling, otherwise a distorted appearance would always result. This contraction varies with different kinds of paste, and requires expert knowledge in the preliminary calculations. The presence of alkalis and iron produces great contraction; silica and silicate of alumina, on the other hand, produce very little. The whole question of contraction, however, is extremely complicated and depends much on the texture of the paste (i.e. whether it is gritty or smooth).

There are various kinds of porcelain, ranging from the 'true' porcelain of the Chinese, the glassy or fritted porcelain of Sèvres, and that of Chelsea and other eighteenth-century factories, to the 'English bone china' which became the accepted formula for almost all English makes during the nineteenth century.

'True' porcelain (which was eventually produced in Europe as well as by the Chinese) consisted of a mixture of petuntse (china-stone) and Kaolin with a glaze of petuntse, to which lime was sometimes added as a softener. 'Glassy' porcelain had a large proportion of frit or glass, together with a little white clay to which a highly fusible glaze was afterwards added. English bone porcelain consisted of a mixture of china-stone and china-clay with the addition of a proportion of bone ash, the glaze being a compound of china-stone and china-clay, with boracic acid, alkalis and lead oxide.

But during the nineteenth century many experiments were made in England with differing kinds of paste, the most notable being the Parian body which has been already referred to in earlier chapters. The chemical basis of this paste was the same as that of 'true porcelain', but the ingredients were combined in different proportions, the felspar of the china-stone being usually in two parts to one part of china-clay. Some of the earlier Parian pieces had additional fusibility given to the paste by an admixture of glass.

Mason's also introduced their famous Ironstone China and various other kinds of semi-porcellanous formulae were evolved in the course of the century; as far as the technique of porcelain making was concerned the Victorian age was indeed extremely progressive, even though the actual styles of the pieces were so frequently based on the great models of the past.

Glossary of Porcelain Terms

Biscuit Ware: Name given to the still undecorated and unglazed articles of porcelain when they have emerged from the first firing and are in a white and porous state.

Body (Paste): The mixture of materials comprising the basic substance of the article.

Bone Ash: The residue from calcined bone, mostly phosphate of lime. 'Bone china' was first perfected in England and it has remained a specially English form of porcelain.

China-clay (Kaolin): Clay in its purest and whitest form, the English kind being derived from Cornwall and Devonshire and consisting of a hydrated silicate of alumina.

China-stone: Rock containing decomposed crystals of felspar with an admixture of glassy quartz. This can be ground into powder and used as the principal fusible constituent of porcelain since it fuses in the heat of the factory furnace. It is the equivalent of the Chinese 'petuntse'.

Colourings: Mineral colours for the decoration of porcelain must be capable of standing the great heat of the firing operations, and they have always been somewhat limited in number. If they are under-glaze they must take the same firing temperature as the glaze; if over-glaze they can be fired at a lower temperature. A third method is the colouring of the actual clay itself, as in the *pâte-sur-pâte* process.

Various metals provide the basis for the colours, cobalt, for instance, giving blues, black, and grey, manganese violet and black, chromium green, antimony yellow and iron red, violet and brown.

Colourings normally have to be combined with a 'flux', i.e. a material which will vitrify in the course of firing and so form a glaze which not only acts as a fixative to the surface of the piece but also becomes a protection to the colours. The colouring may consist of particles of a metallic oxide, or silicates caused by the heat of the firing-oven, as with the blues from cobalt oxide. In some cases the colours are applied before the application of the general glaze; in others, as with enamel colours, they are applied over the glaze, fusing with it and thus forming a firmly fixed body of decoration over the surface.

Contraction under Firing: All forms of both porcelain and pottery undergo a natural contraction in the intense heat of the firing kiln, and this has to be carefully provided for in the original moulding of the pieces. The amount of contraction varies considerably with the nature of the paste, alkalis and iron producing heavy contraction while pastes containing silica or silicate of alumina contract very little.

Enamel Colours: Colouring combined with flux which makes the colours melt into the glaze. Enamels are fired at different temperatures, gold, for instance, requiring a lower temperature than ground colours such as apple-green or Rose Pompadour.

Felspar: The principal ingredient in china stone, occurring in crystalline form which afterwards fuses in the heat of the furnace.

Flambé Glaze: Originally a Chinese style of glazing with a clouded or mottled effect. In Victorian porcelain the term is specially associated with the fine work of Bernard Moore who produced *flambé* glazes of great beauty.

Flux: A form of fusible glass which is combined with the various porcelain colourings to melt them into the glaze.

Frit: A form of glass used to give translucence to what is usually called 'artificial porcelain' (i.e. porcelain which emerges with a glassy or 'fritted' quality).

Gilding: Flux is added to a mixture of mercury and gold, and by the addition of turpentine and oil a gold paint is produced which can be applied direct to the porcelain itself. The piece is then fired in a 'muffle-kiln' and a matt surface of gold decoration obtained. By the process of burnishing (friction caused by rubbing with agate or other polished stone) a brilliant and lustrous surface of gold can be obtained. 'Raised gold', which gives such a splendid finishing touch to any piece, is produced by first applying the design in enamel to the object before it is gilded.

Glaze: The vitreous covering which is given to all porcelain in order to preserve the decoration and to protect the pieces from discoloration, dust, etc. Lead glaze, with a high percentage of lead oxide, was the standard form for many years. Other forms of glaze have been composed of felspar, gypsum, quartz, flint, borax, salt, potash and soda. Coloured glazes can be obtained by adding metal oxides from cobalt, copper, iron, manganese, etc. Salt glaze was used for pottery and stoneware, tin-glaze for majolica. Felspathic glazes are those in which felspathic minerals are the main ingredients.

Glost Oven: The apparatus for the melting of the glaze on to the porcelain so that it is perfectly fused with the body.

Hard Paste: Term generally used to denote porcelain composed of paste which is impervious to the scratch of a steel knife. Neither this, however, nor the companion term 'Soft paste' are really satisfactory.

Ironstone China: A name permanently associated with the firm of Mason's who first marketed it. It was a trade name (i.e. china 'hard as iron') and had no special reference to the presence of ironstone in the paste, though this may have suggested it.

Moulds: Plaster of Paris moulds for making porcelain figures are filled by the workmen with 'slip' (i.e. the paste in a liquid state). The water from the 'slip' is absorbed by the mould, leaving a lining of the paste which can afterwards be removed since it contracts and hardens in the process of drying.

Muffle-kiln: A kiln for firing enamels and gold decoration. The articles are entirely protected from the smoke and flame of the fire by a system of surrounding flues.

Oven: General kiln in which articles are fired, but without the special protection afforded by the muffle-kiln described above. The pieces are, however, placed in 'saggers'.

Parian: A porcelain paste, usually composed of felspar and china clay, which emerges with a resemblance to marble. It was extensively used for figures, groups and busts during the Victorian era.

Pâte-sur-pâte: A form of applied decoration in 'slip' made before any firing of the piece has taken place. (For a fuller description see section on Mintons.)

Potter's Wheel: The disc, or little circular table, placed on a spindle, which was originally rotated by foot-power so as to leave the potter free to use both hands in the shaping of the clay before him. It was in use in China from the earliest times and has always been the foundation tool on to which clay is 'thrown' to be moulded into the desired form. Later forms of the wheel have been, of course, driven by mechanical power.

Propping: The supporting of the more fragile articles during the firing with 'props' of porcelain of the same nature as the pieces themselves, thus acting as a protective scaffolding in the great heat of the kiln. With figures this has always been specially necessary, and though they themselves frequently have supporting accessories, such as trees or rocks or furniture, they still require complicated 'propping' before undergoing the fire. The 'props' are made so as to be easily detachable from the pieces afterwards, and they have to be of exactly the same constituency since they must contract at the same rate in order to preserve the article from distortion.

Pieces of clay called 'stilts' and 'spurs' are also used as a protection for pieces during the glazing in the glost oven. They occasionally leave small marks which show where the pieces have come into contact with them.

Sagger: The vessel in which pieces are placed for general protection while they are being fired in the kilns. The word is also spelt 'saggar' and may have originated as a corruption of 'safeguard'.

Slip: Clay or any other kind of paste mixed with water so that it can be easily moulded into delicate decorative forms and applied to the ware, as in the *pâte-sur-pâte* process.

Soft Paste: Porcelain which can be scratched with a steel knife, as opposed to 'hard paste' which is impervious to it. Like its companion term it is not really satisfactory; so many different kinds of paste were produced during the nineteenth century that the old simple distinction between 'hard' and 'soft' can no longer be made.

Throwing: The act of shaping vases, plates, cups, etc., on the potter's wheel.

Index

INDEX

For the names of porcelain artists see Appendix A, and for technical terms see Glossary, p. 118

Abraham, R., 43
Adams, W. and Son, 68, 83–84
Albert Works, 72
Allen, T., 36, 75
Alloa Works, 85
Armstrong, R., 62, 64
Arnold, M., 22
Arnoux, L., 32
Art Journal, The, 63, 64, 65, 110
Ashworth's, 70, 71

Baldock and Garman, 66
Bancroft, J., 32
Battam, T., 40
Bell's of Glasgow, 85, 103
Belleek, 61, 62–64, 84
Belleuse, C. de, 35, 72
Bemrose, G., 14
Besche, L., 43
Binns, R. W., 47, 48
Bloor, R., 52
Boote, T. and R., 39, 74, 104, 109
Booth's 13, 52, 103
Bott, T., 23, 47
Boullemier, A., 32, 36
Brameld, G. and J., 58
Bridgewood and Son, 72, 79

Brindley, J., 67, 68
Brown-Westhead, Moore and Co. 64–66
Bruffs, The, 45
Byerley, T., 75

Callowhill, J., 48
Cauldon Place, 64–66, 103
Chamberlain's (Worcester), 47, 48
Clarke, E., 72
Coalport, 20, 25, 26, 27, 43–47, 66, 87, 100, 110
Cobridge Works, 81, 103
Copeland's, 20, 25, 39–43, 74, 87, 99–100, 106–7
Copeland, W. T., 39
Cook, W., 45
Crown Staffordshire Co., 13, 77–79
Crown Works, 76

Dale Hall Works, 71
Damage and Repairs, 28–31
Daniell, A. and R., 45
Davenport, 25, 67–69 102
Davenport, J., 67

Derby, 21, 25, 32, 37, 48, 87, 102
Dewsberry (Dewsbury), D., 75, 76
Doulton, 75
Dresden Works, Fenton, 80

Edward VII, 54 (As Prince of Wales, 63, 64)
Edwards, J., 71–72
Exhibition of 1862, 35, 39, 49, 51, 65, 77

Flambé Glazes, 60
Fitzwilliam, Earl, 57, 58
Flight, Barr and Barr, 47
Foley Works, 80
Foster, H., 37
French Exhibition of 1855, 70
Furnival, T. and Sons, 76

Gallimore, W., 61
Garnkirk Works, 24
Garrett, T., 39, 40
'Geisha, The', 21
Gilbert, W. S., 20
Gladstone, W., 54
Godden, G., 98
Goode, T. and Co., 61
Goss, 61
Grand Duchess of Mecklenburg-Strelitz, 42
Grainger's, (Worcester), 41, 47, 48, 50–51, 88
Great Exhibition of 1851, 18, 19, 33, 36, 40, 42, 44, 45, 51, 65, 69. (Also Appendix c)
Green Family, The, 77
Greenfield Works, 80

Hadley, J., 48, 49–50, 51, 101

Hall, S. C., 61
Hancock, G., 32
Hartshorne, J., 45
Harvey Adams and Co., 82
Henk, C., 36, 37
Herculaneum Works, 68
Hicks, Meigh and Johnson, 70
Hilditch and Hopwood, 109
Hill Top Pottery, (Sir James Duke), 81
Hobson, R. L., 50
Hughes, J. L., 37
Hürten, C. F., 43

Ironstone China, (see Mason's)
'Ivanhoe', 22

Jahn, L., 36
Jewitt, L., 61, 65, 66, 69, 81
Japonaiserie and 'Japan' patterns, 28, 47, 48–49, 54–55, 68

Kändler, J., 17
Kauffmann, A., 43
Kerr, W. H., 47, 62
Kidston, R. A., 84
Keys and Mountford, 73
King George V, 54
King William IV, 57, 67
Knight and Rowley, 79

Leroy, D., 56
Lessore, E., 36, 75
Litherland, W., 53
Locke and Co., 51–52
Locker and Co., late Bloor, 53

Madeley, 66–67
Marcolini, Count, 17, 19

Mason's Ironstone China, 70–72, 103, 107–8, 117
Mason, C. J., 70, 77
McBirney, D., 62
McInnes, J., 53
Meigh's (Old Hall Works) 69–70, 103, 108
Meigh, J., 69
Meissen, 17, 20
Meli, G., 73
'Mikado, The', 21
Mintons, 20, 25, 28, 32–39, 66, 67, 73, 75, 80, 88, 92, 99, 105–6
  Acid Gold Process, 37–38
Mountford, J., 40
Moore, Bernard, 60–61, 102
Morley, F., 70
Mussill, W., 36

Nautilus Porcelain Co., 85
Newfield Works, 80
New Town Pottery, 83

Owen, G., 49

Parian, 25, 35, 39–41, 51, 69, 72–74, 117
Paris Exhibitions, 1867, 48, 49
  1889, 42, 43
'Patience', 20
Pâte-sur-pâte, 33–34
Philadelphia Exhibition, 1876, 38, 39
Phillips, E., 53
Pinxton, 66
Porcelaine Opaque, 18, 72
Powell and Bishop, 77

Presswell, J., 58
Protat, H., 36
Pugin, A., 22, 38
Queen Victoria, 33, 45, 53, 54, 62, 111
Queen Mary, 53, 54
'Quentin Durward', 22

Randall, J., 26, 44
Randall, T. M., 66–67
Registration Marks, 88–89
Reuter, E., 36, 37
Ridgways, 64–65, 108
Robinson and Chapman, 79
Robinson and Leadbeater, 73
Rockingham, 56–59, 104, 109
Rothschild, Baron, 20
Rose, J., 44, 46
Rose, W., 44
'Rose Pompadour' ('Rose du Barri') 20, 23, 26, 27, 28, 41, 44, 47, 65, 66, 67,

Samson, 78
'Sang-de-Boeuf' glaze, 60
Schenk, F., 80
Scott, Sir W., 22
Sèvres, 17, 20, 26, 27, 28, 33, 36, 37, 43, 44, 45, 46, 48, 56, 57, 62, 66, 67,
Shaw, N., 20
Sheridan Works, Longton, 81–82
Solon, M. L., 32, 33–34, 80, 92
Sotheby's, 35
Spode (*See under* Copeland's)
Stevenson and Hancock, 53
Swinton (*See under* Rockingham)
Sutherland, D. and Sons, 79

Tennyson, Lord, 22

Trent Pottery, (George Jones), 73, 80

Verreville Pottery, 84

Waddesdon Manor, 20

Wall, Dr., 17, 47, 52

Weaver, J., 43

Wedgwood, 34, 75, 108

Wentworth House, 58

Whistler, J., 49

Wilde, O., 20

Worcester (The Royal Porcelain Works), 17, 18, 21, 23, 25, 28, 41, 47–50, 53, 62, 78, 88, 101, 109

Wornum, R., 110–11

Wright, A., 37